Krakow

WHAT'S NEW | WHAT'S ON | WHAT'S BEST

www.timeout.com/krakow

Contents

Published by Time Out Guides Ltd
Universal House
251 Tottenham Court Road
London W1T 7AB
Tel: + 44 (0)20 7813 3000
Fax: + 44 (0)20 7813 6001
Email: guides@timeout.com
www.timeout.com

Managing Director Peter Fiennes
Editorial Director Ruth Jarvis
Business Manager Dan Allen
Editorial Manager Holly Pick
Assistant Management Accountant Ija Krasnikova

Time Out Guides is a wholly owned subsidiary of Time Out Group Ltd.

© **Time Out Group Ltd**
Chairman Tony Elliott
Chief Executive Officer David King
Group General Manager/Director Nichola Coulthard
Time Out Communications Ltd MD David Pepper
Time Out International Ltd MD Cathy Runciman
Time Out Magazine Ltd Publisher/Managing Director Mark Elliott
Production Director Mark Lamond
Group IT Director Simon Chappell
Head of Marketing Catherine Demajo

Time Out and the Time Out logo are trademarks of Time Out Group Ltd.

This edition first published in Great Britain in 2009 by Ebury Publishing
A Random House Group Company
Company information can be found on www.randomhouse.co.uk
Random House UK Limited Reg. No. 954009
10 9 8 7 6 5 4 3 2 1

Distributed in the US by Publishers Group West
Distributed in Canada by Publishers Group Canada

For further distribution details, see www.timeout.com

ISBN: 978-1-84670-125-2

A CIP catalogue record for this book is available from the British Library.

Printed and bound in Germany by Appl.

The Random House Group Limited supports The Forest Stewardship Council (FSC), the
leading international forest certification organisation. All our titles that are printed on
Greenpeace approved FSC certified paper carry the FSC logo. Our paper procurement
policy can be found at www.rbooks.co.uk/environment.

Time Out carbon-offsets all its flights with Trees for Cities (www.treesforcities.org).

Krakow Shortlist

The **Time Out Krakow Shortlist 2009** is one of a new series of guides that draws on Time Out's background as a magazine publisher to keep you current with everything that's going on in town. As well as Krakow's key sights and the best of its eating, drinking and leisure options, it picks out the most exciting venues to have opened recently and gives a full, year-round calendar of events. It also includes features on the important news, trends and openings, all compiled by locally based editors and writers. Whether you're visiting for the first time in your life or the first time this year, you'll find the *Time Out Krakow Shortlist* contains everything you need to know, in a portable and easy-to-use format.

The guide divides central Krakow into six areas, each containing listings for Sights & Museums, Eating & Drinking, Shopping, Nightlife and Arts & Leisure, and maps pinpointing their locations. At the front of the book are chapters rounding up these scenes city-wide, and giving a shortlist of our overall picks. We also include itineraries for days out, plus essentials such as transport information and hotels.

Our listings give phone numbers as dialled within Krakow. From abroad, use your country's exit code followed by 48 (the country code for Poland) and the number given, dropping the initial '0'.

We have noted price categories by using one to four złoty signs (Z-ZZZZ), representing budget, moderate, expensive and luxury. Major credit cards are accepted unless otherwise stated. We also indicate when a venue is NEW.

All our listings are double-checked, but businesses do sometimes close or change their hours or prices, so it's a good idea to call a venue before visiting. While every effort has been made to ensure accuracy, the publishers cannot accept responsibility for any errors that this guide may contain.

Venues are marked on the maps using symbols numbered according to their order within the chapter and colour-coded according to the type of venue they represent:

1 Sights & Museums
1 Eating & Drinking
1 Shopping
1 Nightlife
1 Arts & Leisure

Map key	
Major sight or landmark	⬛
Railway station	⬛
Park	⬛
College/hospital	⬛
Neighbourhood	STRADOM
Pedestrian street	▭
Main road	—
Church	✚
Airport	✈

Time Out Krakow Shortlist

EDITORIAL

Editor Peterjon Cresswell
Proofreader Tamsin Shelton

DESIGN

Art Director Scott Moore
Art Editor Pinelope Kourmouzoglou
Senior Designer Henry Elphick
Graphic Designers Kei Ishimaru,
  Nicola Wilson
Advertising Designer Jodi Sher
Picture Editor Jael Marschner
Deputy Picture Editor Lynn Chambers
Picture Researcher Gemma Walters
Picture Desk Assistant Marżena Żoładż
Picture Librarian Christina Theisen

ADVERTISING

Commercial Director Mark Phillips
International Advertising Manager
  Kasimir Berger
International Sales Executive
  Charlie Sokol
Advertising Sales (Krakow)
  Cracow-Life.com

MARKETING

Marketing Manager Yvonne Poon
**Sales & Marketing Director, North
  America & Latin America** Lisa Levinson
Senior Publishing Brand Manager
  Luthfa Begum
Marketing Designers Anthony Huggins

PRODUCTION

Production Manager Brendan McKeown
Production Controller Damian Bennett
Production Co-ordinator Kelly Fenlon

CONTRIBUTORS

This guide was researched and written by Peterjon Cresswell with contributions from Piotr Art, Robin Das, Nicholas Hodge and Marcin Wojtaszek. The editor would like to thank Ewa Binkin (Polish National Tourist Office, UK), Mark Bradshaw (Cracow-Life.com), Marcin Drobisz (Krakow Tourist Office), www.krakow-apartments.com and Leszek Werenowski.

PHOTOGRAPHY

All photography by Fumie Suzuki except: pages 58, 59, 72, 73, 109, 115, 131 Marzena Zoladz; page 126 Pawel Sawicki, Auschwitz-Birkena.

The following images were provided by the featured establishments/artists: 11, 29, 30, 31, 64, 76, 127, 128, 129, 130, 135.

Cover photograph: Rynek Glowny. Credit: Getty Images

MAPS

Maps by JS Graphics Ltd. (john@jsgraphics.co.uk).
The maps are based on material supplied by ITMB Publishing Ltd.

About Time Out

Founded in 1968, Time Out has expanded from humble London beginnings into the leading resource for those wanting to know what's happening in the world's greatest cities. As well as our influential what's-on weeklies in London, New York and Chicago, we publish more than a dozen other listings magazines in cities as varied as Beijing and Mumbai. The magazines established Time Out's trademark style: sharp writing, informed reviewing and bang up-to-date inside knowledge of every scene.

Time Out made the natural leap into travel guides in the 1980s with the City Guide series, which now extends to over 50 destinations around the world. Written and researched by expert local writers and generously illustrated with original photography, the full-size guides cover a larger area than our Shortlist guides and include many more venue reviews, along with additional background features and a full set of maps.

Throughout this rapid growth, the company has remained proudly independent, still owned by Tony Elliott four decades after he started Time Out London as a single fold-out sheet of A5 paper. This independence extends to the editorial content of all our publications, this Shortlist included. No establishment has been featured because it has advertised, and no payment has influenced any of our reviews. And, for our critics, there's definitely no such thing as a free lunch: all restaurants and bars are visited and reviewed anonymously, and Time Out always picks up the bill.

For more about the company, see www.timeout.com.

Don't Miss

Krakow History Museum p51

Sights & Museums

History is what brings many to Krakow – tourists, historians, filmmakers. Some are drawn to the city's tragic role as headquarters of Nazi Poland, flocking to the Jewish hub of Kazimierz, the wartime ghetto of Podgórze just over the river and, within close range, Auschwitz (p125) itself. Others are happy just to wander around the pristine Old Town, its buildings relatively untouched by the war or subsequent Socialism, perhaps calling in at a museum or two.

The only must-sees are St Mary's Basilica (p52) and Wawel Cathedral and Castle (p96). Baroque churches abound, and the art treasures kept in the Wyspiański (p54), Czartoryski (p49) and National Museums (p120) merit a visit for anyone staying longer than a day.

Giving access to all branches of the National Museum, St Mary's and two dozen other venues, plus free city transport, the Krakow Card (www.krakowcard.com) is sold around town for 24 and 48 hours (50zł/65zł). Note that most museums charge an extra fee if you would like to take photographs – a steward may stop you snapping if not. Entry to Jewish sights, particularly cemeteries, requires male visitors to wear a yarmulke skullcap, dished out at the entrance.

Only in Krakow can you find the legacy of the Modernist Młoda Polska trend of the late 1800s – in café (Jama Michalika p60), museum (National, Wyspiański, Józef Mehoffer p117), gallery (Palace of Art p51), theatre (Stary p74) and church (Franciscan; p50) form.

walkable Old Town. Starting at the main market square, Rynek Główny (p34), a sight in itself, you can gawp at St Mary's Basilica (altar opening at 11.45am, not Sundays), climb the Town Hall Tower (summer only), browse the stalls in the Cloth Hall (p49) and pop into St Adalbert's Church (p52). After 2010, two of the three city-centre branches of the National Museum, upstairs in the Cloth Hall, and the Krakow History Museum (p51) on the corner of the market square, will have been revamped and reopened. The lesser known third branch, the Burgher House (p49), is a reconstruction of how locals lived 400 years ago.

North of here, the Czartoryski, with its Da Vinci and assorted historic artefacts, is a popular attraction; the nearby Pharmacy Museum (p51) sadly isn't but should be. Immediately west stands

Man-made mounds, old (Krak's p102) and modern (Piłsudski p130), are another local peculiarity.

Krakow is the starting point for trips to Wieliczka (p127) salt mine and Auschwitz concentration camp – any number of tour companies in town provide coach trips and guided commentary. In and around Krakow you'll also find city walking tours, cycle tours, bar crawling tours, tours of Nowa Huta (p40) by Trabant car, tours of farms, tours of Jewish or Gypsy culture, tours by golf buggy, skiing tours of the Tatras and tailor-made tours of all varieties. Vantage points to get your bearings include the Town Hall Tower (p52) in the main square, Wawel and the Klub Panorama (p96) bar atop the Jubilat shopping centre.

Old Town

With the exception of Wawel, nearly all of Krakow's main attractions are contained in the

SHORTLIST

Best recent reopening
- Bishop Erazm Ciołek Palace (p49)

Best panorama
- Town Hall Tower (p52)

Most wow factor
- St Mary's Basilica (p52)
- Wawel Cathedral (p96)

Best Da Vinci
- Czartoryski Museum (p49)

Most visited tourist sight
- Wieliczka (p127)

Most unusual attraction
- Nowa Huta (p40)

Most moving sights
- Auschwitz (p125)
- Silesia House (p113)

Best historic artefact
- Collegium Maius (p50)

the Collegium Maius (p50), with its artefacts related to Copernicus' groundbreaking studies here; further are the Wyspiański and National Museums. South of the main square, the Royal Route down Grodzka leads to a cluster of churches, including early Baroque Sts Peter & Paul (p49). This is the ecclesiastical quarter where Pope John Paul II lived and worked, as evidenced in the rather obsessive Archdiocesan Museum (p45). The Bishop Erazm Ciołek Palace (p49), the most significant local museum reopening of late, is a more worthwhile visit on the same cobbled street. Medieval Polish and Orthodox art are presented in a gorgeous 15th-century building. A neglected Archaeology Museum (p45) here is also worth a look-in.

Wawel & wartime sights

Divided between Cathedral and Castle, hilltop Wawel is Poland's national treasure, a collection of museums, tombs and treasures within fortified walls as sacred as Westminster Abbey or Notre-Dame. Don't miss the Cathedral and, if you can, catch the Crown Treasury (p95; closed Mondays, Sundays in winter). Allow half a day to explore here – there are restaurants, toilets, little pressure to buy souvenirs and a post office to send postcards.

Wawel overlooks the Jewish hub of Kazimierz, whose synagogues are now nearly all museums but whose culture is being revived in the form of cultural festivals, galleries, restaurants and shops. There are Christian churches here too, plus random attractions such as the Ethnographic Museum (p79), City Engineering Museum (p76) and a new Aquarium (p76), the latter in Stradom but outside the Old Town on the Kazimierz side.

Opposite, Podgórze easily earns the epithet 'up and coming', with its new business hotel, bars and eateries – but most cross the river for the wartime sights (the Jewish Ghetto, the Schindler Factory p104, Płaszów p102) they would have seen in *Schindler's List*.

Manggha p95

Ancora p54

Eating & Drinking

According to Adam Chrzątowski, head of Ancora (p54), 'Poland has fine game, forest fruits and river fish but cooking techniques hadn't changed since the war'. This was how the contemporary master chef described the status quo before he launched his venue.

After 40 years of shortages and neglect, and ten years of recovery, Krakow is now moving with the times. The density of venues in the Old Town means competition is stiff. A sloppy place won't last long. A significant number of chefs, cooks and waitstaff have gained hands-on experience in the UK and Ireland, and returned with skills and positive attitudes – service here will be better than you'll find in Prague or Budapest.

And as for those ingredients, you'll see them most used to recreate classic Polish dishes in historic dining settings, some kind of wild-berry accompaniment to venison in a place such as Pod Aniołami (p65), Hawełka (p60) or Wentzl (p66). Beetroot, cabbage and potatoes feature in the local soups, a delicacy when carefully prepared. Desserts are another speciality, cheesecake or pancakes, both usually brimming with fresh fruit.

All well and good. But still far too few establishments in Krakow are pushing the envelope any further than this. Tourists will be fed, satisfied, sated – but rarely challenged. Ancora, and hopefully others to follow, are setting about changing all that.

YOU KNOW WHO YOU ARE.

KRAKOW • PL. MARIACKI 9.
48 12 429 11 55 • HARDROCK.COM

Hard Rock
CAFE

If only restaurateurs could take a few leads from bar owners. The Krakow drinking scene, centred on the main streets (Floriańska, Sławkowska, Szewska) leading off the main market square and, most of all, plac Nowy in Kazimierz, is as lively and as varied as you'll find anywhere in Eastern Europe. The Old Town has always been thick with bars, once dark, smoky cellars, now contemporary spots and DJ bars. Plac Nowy is also a recent phenomenon – only a decade ago, this grey market square contained little but empty stalls. Now it is lined with 15 bars, most notably instigators Alchemia (p82) and Singer (p87). A recent overspill into Podgórze over the river includes seminal Drukarnia (p107).

You can also find vodka bars (Baroque, p55; Starka, p87), cocktail bars (Paparazzi, p65) and wine bars (Vinoteka La Bodega, p66).

Timings, types & tips

The average *restauracja* opens late morning and operates to late evening. A cheap neighbourhood place, traditionally serving either dumplings (*pierogi*) or pancakes (*naleśniki*), with a range of fillings and sauces, will open earlier and close around 7pm. At more contemporary venues, the kitchen should stay open until 11pm. Some places close on Sundays but you'll still find scores of busy restaurants around the Old Town.

Most menus will feature English translations. Appetisers could be a plate of herring or cold meat, followed by the Polish strong suit of soups. Beetroot soup, *barszcz*, and *żurek*, rye soup with sausage and egg, are invariably included, but you might also find *krupnik* barley and potato soup with meaty chunks and *cebulowa*, onion soup. A basket of white, brown or rye bread will be placed alongside.

SHORTLIST

Best new venues
- Wesele (p66)

Best contemporary
- Ancora (p54)

Best Italian
- Aqua e Vino (p54)

Best Jewish
- Rubinstein (p84)

Best place for your parents
- Miód Malina (p62)

Best cheap Polish
- Bar Grodzki (p55)

Best regional Polish
- Jarema (p114)
- Morskie Oko (p63)

Best for fish
- Farina (p59)

Best river view
- Hotel Poleski (p96)

Wentzl p66

DON'T MISS

Get the local experience

Over 50 of the world's top destinations available.

Vinoteka La Bodega p66

Meat features heavily in the main courses, usually pork, chicken or beef, in a thick sauce, accompanied by potatoes, rice and/or a heap of cabbage. The better establishments will concoct a flavouring made with berries or fruit. Fish options are usually limited to trout or carp.

Vegetarians now have plenty of choice in Krakow's international outlets (the Georgian chain Gruzińskie Chaczapuri, p60; quality pizzerias), but in domestic eateries they may be limited to pancakes or *pierogi* filled with local cheese or forest mushrooms.

Desserts are another speciality, cheesecake (perhaps served warm with ice-cream), fruit pies and gooey cakes. Fresh, seasonal fruit is another attractive option.

Unless you hit the top bracket, restaurants are reasonably priced, and it's good form to round up the bill by a few złotys at the end.

Lurid beers & hot drinks

Coffee here is decent these days – gone are the days of grainy gruel. Nearly all cafés and many restaurants provide offer a full range of fruit and herbal teas.

All bars will serve one or two local beers on draught (Żywiec, Okocim, Tyskie, EB), some with a dark variant, either in a half-litre glass (*duże*) or 33cl (*mało*). One local peculiarity that later spread across Poland is for the barman to flavour the beer with syrup, usually raspberry (*malina*), perhaps cherry (*wiśnia*), even ginger (*imbirowy*). The fashion started in the early 1990s to attract more women to drink. Locals of both sexes also drink beer through straws – don't be offended if you're offered one with your pint.

In winter, mulled wine and mulled beer feature on many drinks menus, both flavoured with spices.

Vodkas come in many flavours – only foreigners and uncouth youngsters mix them with fruit juice. The better local brands – Wyborowa, Starka, Cracovia – produce in various strengths and flavours. Look out for Żubrówka bison-grass vodka and the sweet, cherry-flavoured Wiśniówka.

Fruit juices also come in cherry, blackcurrant and other sweet flavours, along with the standard apple, orange, and so on.

Breakfasts & snacks

Hotel breakfasts are usually of decent quality – you may even find marinated peppers, herring or salmon among the standard cheese, jam and hams. Many places in the Old Town, and on and around plac Nowy, also do breakfast – at Les Couleurs (p83) it's stylish and continental; at Metropolitan (p62) it can be substantial and comes in global varieties.

Although you'll find the usual takeaway pizzas and kebabs – locals pace their evening at plac Nowy by the toasted baguettes served until late from hatches in the market building – all over town you'll see dinky see-through stands selling the local staple *obwarzanki*, half-bagels, half-pretzels, dotted with either sesame or poppy seeds, for about 1.30zł.

Hawełka p60

Cloth Hall p68

Shopping

Malls, markets, traditional family-run boutiques and global chains, all within a short walk of each other, offer plenty of choice and convenience around downtown Krakow. With the opening of a 270-outlet mall by the main station, then one in Kazimierz, nearly all international brands now have a store in the city, while most of the Old Town seems like one long shop-window display of pretty chocolates, bright jewellery and arty galleries.

Although there is no market in the city centre – unless you count the leatherware and woodcraft souvenirs laid out in rows in the centrepiece Cloth Hall (p68) – a short walk away are the markets of Kleparz, ideal spots to browse for local cheeses, dried fruits and vodkas. For Christmas, stalls set up around the main square itself.

What to buy where

Amber and original jewellery are a Krakow speciality, a hangover from the days when the city was an inland member of the Hanseatic League. Walk down Floriańska and you'll see at least a dozen outlets, where you can also pick up a necklace, bracelet or charm made from a locally found precious stone or mineral. This main shopping drag also contains a number of antique stores and galleries where auctions are held.

Around the Cloth Hall, the main square features drinks stores and chocolatiers (Wedel p70, Wawel),

Wanted. Jumpers, coats and people with their knickers in a twist.

From the people who feel moved to bring us their old books and CDs, to the people fed up to the back teeth with our politicians' track record on climate change, Oxfam supporters have one thing in common. They're passionate. If you've got a little fire in your belly, we'd love to hear from you. Visit us at **oxfam.org.uk**

Be Humankind Oxfam

bookshops (Księgarnia Hetmańska p69) and music shops (Kurant p69) barely changed since 1989. The corner by St Adalbert's Church has more high-end shops, most notably at Pasaż 13 (p70), an upscale centre tastefully fitted into a historic passageway by luxury-hotel group Likus. Along with its own Likus Concept Store (p70; fashion brands, wines, olive oils, meats, cheeses), you'll be able to browse Benetton, Rossignol, L'Occitane and local menswear outlet Vistula (p70).

Nearby Hexeline (p69) is the equally classy equivalent for locally designed ladieswear. If you're looking for something more radical and contemporary, Punkt (p70) should be your first port of call. Designer/artist Monika Drożiński is the brightest talent to have emerged recently.

For funky finds for the home, Galeria Dom Polski (p69), Galeria Osobliwości (p69) and Galeria

SHORTLIST

Best contemporary fashion
- Punkt (p70)

Best selection of vodkas
- Szambelan (p70)

Best for second-hand vinyl
- High Fidelity (p89)

Best produce market
- Lea market (p122)

Best bookshop
- Massolit Books & Café (p122)

Best amber
- Galeria RA/Baltic Amber (p69)

Easiest souvenir shopping
- Cloth Hall (p68)

Wackiest gifts
- Galeria Osobliwości (p69)

Most authentic mementos
- Galeria Plakatu (p69)

DON'T MISS

Stary Kleparz p115

Plakatu (p69) should provide you with ornaments, exotic items and old theatre posters respectively. If you're just after a present or wedding gift, then Alhena (p68) carries the finest Polish cut glass.

New books, guides, DVDs and all kinds of stationery can be found at Empik (p68) on the main market square. Krakow isn't that big on second-hand record and bookstores. Vinyl is only available by the meticulously catalogued boxload in High Fidelity (p89), down a Kazimierz backstreet. For English-language novels, histories and guides, many related to Poland or the region, Massolit Books & Café (p122) is one of the finest outlets of its type in Europe. Flea markets aren't big here – for that you'll have to go to Warsaw, and the huge one by the old national sports stadium.

For food and drink, you'll either have to hit Galeria Krakowska (p114) or individual stores – there isn't really a one-stop supermarket in the city centre. For gifts and souvenirs, Szambelan (p70) sells vodkas in every kind of flavour; Kopernik Toruńskie Pierniki (p69) proffers local gingerbread, and Wedel sweets and chocolate.

Service & payment

Shops in the city centre usually open six days a week, many on Sundays too. Most open at 9am or 10am and close between 7pm and 9pm. The national holidays when most close are: New Year's Day; Easter Sunday; Easter Monday; 1 and 3 May; Pentecost; Corpus Christi; 15 August; 1 and 11 November; 25 and 26 December. The concept of January or summer sales has not yet caught on in most stores around town.

Credit cards are accepted almost everywhere. Euros are also taken at some high-end boutiques – otherwise payment is in local złotys. Service is generally good and most shop assistants under 40 speak at least reasonable English. Goods are carefully packaged and wrapped, and presented with a smile and a thank you.

Galeria RA/Baltic Amber p69

Baroque p55

Nightlife

After dark, Krakow is livelier than almost any city of its size in the region – although it has no big disco or superclub. Action tends to take place in bars and smaller venues, capable of accommodating DJs and modest live acts. Krakow has promoted and hosted jazz for many years, with half-a-dozen spots on and around the main market square.

The one key spot if you just want to let loose for the night is a bar-filled building just outside the Old Town in the Stradom district at Wielopole 15 (p88). Started up in 2002, this now contains arguably the two best bar-clubs in town, Kitsch (p89) and Łubu-Dubu (p90), plus two others worth investigating as you pop in and out of each venue

on the same staircase. Entry is free or the admission fee nominal if a live act has been booked.

New spots & old haunts

The management of Kitsch and housemate Caryca has just a new venue nearby, Circus. Although yet to be welcomed into the fold as warmly as Wielopole 15 and preferred Old Town hotspots have been, Circus doesn't follow the cramped, dimly lit, cellar model but has filled the ample space of a former cinema with bright lights, sparkling decor and bizarre animals. The dance sounds are fun if not particularly adventurous.

The same goes for DJing in other downtown hubs. Where Bracka meets the main market square,

Discover the city from your back pocket

Essential for your weekend break, 25 top cities available.

there are bars and clubs on opposite sides of the street, the most popular being Rdza (p73). Similarly, on Szewska towards the main square, nightspots include Music Bar 9 and recently opened, glitzier Frantic (p72). Within a short walk are Pauza (p72) and Piękny Pies (p72), both bars with a strong DJ element in the basement. On Gołębie, the little triangle of Migrena (p62) and adjoining bar, Cztery Pokoje (p71) opposite, and Boom Bar Rush in the same building, should keep everyone entertained into the small hours.

Kazimierz has clubs too: the main gay venue of Klub Cocon (p90); live music (mainly grunge) at the Kawiarnia Naukowa (p90), and a mix of DJs and gigs at face2face (p89), the key opening of 2008. Its location away from the nightlife vortex of plac Nowy and adjoining streets may prove difficult to woo punters its way on a regular basis,

SHORTLIST

Best retro decor
- Łubu-Dubu (p90)

Best for domestic DJs
- Kijów Club (p124)
- Rdza (p73)

Best for gay clubbers
- Kitsch (p89)
- Klub Cocon (p90)

Best new arrival
- face2face (p89)

Best to impress
- Enso (p122)
- M Club (p72)

Best for a foxy night out
- Cień (p71)
- Frantic (p72)

Best late-night bars with dancefloors
- Pauza (p72)
- Piękny Pies (p72)

Łubu-Dubu p90

but the music programme there looks promising so far.

More established dance clubs include Kijów (p124) west of the Old Town, Cień (p71) near the Floriańska Gate and the weekend-only and chic Enso (p122) in the burgeoning University Quarter.

Although there are only a couple of venues in the neighbourhood at the moment, the area immediately over the river from Kazimierz, Podgórze, should be buzzing with a few new nightspots before too long. The popularity of Drukarnia (p107), jazz bar and after-dark hangout, will not have gone unnoticed as many seek to make returns on investing in Krakow's new-found status as a place of entertainment.

Tips & timings

Some places in the Old Town operate more as pick-up joints. They are not red-light venues per se but the weekend influx of beer monsters from the UK encourages the oldest trade to kick into action. Doormen are placed at some

entrances around the Old Town, perhaps on plac Nowy on a busy night, but security is rarely tight or oppressive. Frisking is almost unheard of.

Similarly, dress codes are only enforced at chic spots such as M Club (p72) and Enso. Unless you're out to impress, smart-casual should get you in to most places.

During the week you shouldn't have to fork out an entrance fee anywhere – unless it's for a special event. A fairly nominal admission is charged at weekends at a handful of venues but drink prices rarely rise above the norm. Happy hours are becoming a more established form of promotion.

For information on concerts and DJ nights, refer to www.Cracow-Life.com or keep a look out for posters and flyers at bars such as Baroque (p55), Dym (p59), Prowincja (p65) or the Budda Bar Drink & Garden (p71). Also around town, the free listings pamphlet www.e-krakow.com is a handy resource every month.

Budda Bar Drink & Garden p71

ARS Cinema p73

Arts & Leisure

Krakow is the cultural capital of Poland. Home of Roman Polanski, Andrzej Wajda, the Młoda Polska movement of the early 20th century and the Grupa Krakowska either side of the war, Krakow has always been big on art, film, theatre, literature and jazz music. Cabaret too – the arts scene of the early 1900s and the post-war period were centred on the Zielony Balonik at the Jama Michalika café, and the Piwnica pod Baranami on the main square. In both cases, artists met to exchange ideas in a liberal atmosphere, authority was mocked and questioned, and everyone had a rare old time.

Polanski (who left Krakow as a boy during the Nazi occupation) and Wajda (a non-local who came

here to study and ended up as one of the city's most influential cultural figures) are well known outside of Poland's borders. Others – theatre director and set designer Tadeusz Kantor, sci-fi writer Stanisław Lem and, above all, painter, playwright and architect Stanisław Wyspiański – are big names in Poland.

In the most recent developments, Krakow at last has a quality, state-of-the-art Opera House (p115), opened in December 2008 after decades of dallying. Three months earlier, Kraftwerk played at the vast, mainly unused steel factory complex at Nowa Huta, as the local Sacrum Profanum Festival rose considerably in profile. Earlier that summer, Underworld performed in

Make the most of London life

front of Krakow's main train station. Hit Krakow at the right time, and you won't go short of arts events to write home about.

Language & performance

The most accessible art forms for the non-Polish speaker coming to Krakow are music and art. The quality of classical music on offer is on a par with most cities of similar size in Germany or Austria. Along with the Opera House, there are the Krakow Philharmonic (p124) and Krakow Chamber Opera (p90). Although Krakow is usually not a stop for major rock bands on their European tour, the summer festivals allow some name acts to perform. For local groups, the Kawiarnia Naukowa (p90) and the recently opened face2face (p90) are the places. Jazz has always been big and half-a-dozen venues (U Muniaka, Harris Piano Jazz Bar, Stalowe Magnolie; p74) stage regular if not nightly shows close to each other around the main square. The annual Krakow Jazz Festival (www.cracjazz.com) on the square is the major music event.

The art scene is harder to follow but keep an eye on Podgórze, the district over the river from Kazimierz, where a network of galleries is expanding around the market square and Węgierska.

There isn't much in town by way of English-language theatre – the Juliusz Słowacki (p74) is a lovely place to watch a famous work even if you can't understand each line of the dialogue. Readings are staged in English in the smaller rooms.

Cinematic tradition

Given the star names who have lived, studied or filmed in Krakow, it is no wonder that cinema is singularly important to the life of the city. Some will recognise locations here from *Schindler's List*.

SHORTLIST

Most prestigious opening
- Krakow Opera (p115)

Best venue for local bands
- Kawiarnia Naukowa (p90)

Most sumptuous cinema
- Kino pod Baranami (p74)

Best music festival
- Sacrum Profanum (p30)

Most ornate theatre
- Juliusz Słowacki Theatre (p74)

Best jazz spots
- Harris Piano Jazz Bar (p74)
- U Muniaka (p74)

Best cabaret venue
- Piwnica pod Baranami (p74)

Most intimate arena
- Krakow Chamber Opera (p90)

Best late-night music venue
- Showtime (p73)

Showtime p73

Kawiarnia Naukowa p90

Others will be disappointed to see no record in Podgórze of Roman Polanski having lived there as a child – although he talks about it a lot in his autobiography, *Roman by Polanski*.

Today Krakow contains a number of multiplexes – including Multikino (p115) and Cinema City (p108) – and a plucky pack of independent movie houses, some historic. Kino pod Baranami (p74) is a sumptuous old palace on the main square that champions the best in world cinema, while ARS Cinema (p73) has four screening rooms, one an old ballroom. Both host imaginative programmes throughout the year, with many seasons for devoted cinephiles.

The festival count seems to grow every year, yet two stalwarts remain at the top of the roster: the Krakow Film Festival (www.kff.com), running since 1961, sees scores of filmmakers descend on the city in late May in the hope of winning a coveted silver or golden dragon. Most of the action takes place at the redoubtable Kijów, which has the biggest screen in town. Short films, documentaries and animation are the main focus. Also worthy of investigation is the Etiuda & Anima Festival (http://etiudaandanima.com) which takes place in November.

Tickets & schedules

Cinema tickets are easily affordable and nearly all big films are shown in original language with Polish subtitles. For other information on arts events, the monthly *Karnet* in Polish and English is the best source. The City Information Point at Św Jana 2 (012 421 77 87, www.karnet.krakow.pl) is also a useful resource, while the outlet at Empik (p68) on the main square sells tickets for all cultural events, including big rock concerts.

Calendar

Christmas market p32

These are the pick of the events staged in Krakow over the year. Festivals have been key to the city's revival, notably the Jewish Culture Festival in Kazimierz (p81).

February

25-28 (2010) **Sea Shanties**
Various locations
www.shanties.pl
Exponents Zejman i Garkumpel play with 30 acts around maritime exhibits.

March

Late Mar **Bach Days**
Various locations
www.amuz.krakow.pl
A series of concerts organised by the local Academy of Music.

April

Early Apr **Culture for Tolerance**
Various locations
www.tolerancja.org.pl
Films, seminars and workshops organised by the local gay community.

May

May **Photomonth**
Various locations
www.photomonth.com
This month-long event involves exhibitions, talks and slide shows in galleries, public spaces and even people's private flats.

Early May **Juwenalia**
Various locations
www.juwenalia.krakow.pl
This week-long equivalent of Rag Week features a series of high-profile domestic rock concerts around the city.

Late May **International Soup Festival**
Plac Nowy, Kazimierz
www.teatrkto.pl
Chefs gather around plac Nowy over the course of a Sunday to concoct their favourite soups, dished out while live acts perform – both for free.

Sacred sounds

Kraftwerk

Easily the most ambitious of Krakow's many music festivals, September's **Sacrum Profanum** complements some of the world's most creative exponents of modern classical music with Krakow's most interesting concert spaces. The term 'classical' is a broad one – Sacrum Profanum is by no means staid, having staged Kraftwerk, Kurt Weill and music by Stockhausen all in the same week at the most recent happening.

2008 was in fact a high point in the festival's six-year history. Having started as the autumn counterpart to Easter's Misteria Paschalia classical festival, Sacrum Profanum has grown exponentially from a modest four-day event of four concerts to staging Kraftwerk over three nights at the gargantuan Nowa Huta steelworks, and the music of Karlheinz Stockhausen at the Schindler Factory.

Ex-industrial concert spaces are one thing – the Schindler Factory (see box p103) is where Ghetto Jews were saved from the Nazi death camps by the owner of the same name. Stockhausen's music was partly inspired by his own mother's death at the hands of the Nazis. Stockhausen had died the year before, and this particular concert of 2008 was perhaps the most moving performance in the history of the event.

Each year is given over to the music of one country or region. After France and Russia, the choice of America in 2007 saw the musical agenda take a more avant-garde approach, a policy that was continued in 2008 – and now into 2009 when Britain comes into focus.

Festival programmers have invited several acts to come over, including Cinematic Orchestra, born out of Ninja Tunes, Coventry's Brian Ferneyhough of the New Complexity school and contemporary chamber orchestra London Sinfonietta. Performances will be from 13 to 19 September. The Nowa Huta steelworks will again be used, with perhaps some new concert spaces to be uncovered amid the abandoned buildings of Podgórze.

Late May-early June
Krakow Film Festival
Kijów Cinema, p124
& other locations
www.kff.com.pl
The KFF attracts the biggest names in Poland whose features, shorts and documentaries are screened at a number of venues. Prizes are themed around Krakow's signature dragon.

June

Ongoing Krakow Film Festival
(see May).

Late June-early July
Jewish Culture Festival
Kazimierz
www.jewishfestival.pl
This biggest event has grown from humble beginnings in 1989. See p81.

July

Ongoing Jewish Culture Festival
(see June).

5-31 (2009)
Summer Jazz Festival
Piwnica pod Baranami, p74
www.cracjazz.com
Three weeks of daily jazz concerts take place in this cabaret venue, spilling on to the main square for the grand finale.

Early July **International Street Theatre Festival**
Various locations
www.teatrkto.pl
Circus acts, comedians and buskers give free shows in public spaces.

August

15-31 (2009) **Music in Old Cracow Festival**
Krakow Philharmonic, p124
& other locations
www.capellacracoviensis.pl
Organised by Capella Cracoviensis, the renowned local orchestra who specialise in Polish music through the ages, this 17-day event is held at similarly historic venues in town.

Mid Aug **Pierogi Festival**
Maly Rynek
www.biurofestiwalowe.pl
A two-day celebration of Poland's humble dumpling climaxes with the public awarding of the Casimir Prize for the best new variety. Stalls are set up around the Maly Rynek.

21-22 (2009) **Coke Live Music Festival**
Krakow Aviation Museum, Nowa Huta
www.livefestival.pl
Krakow's biggest rock festival is this two-day bash at the outdoor Aviation Museum near Nowa Huta. Recent headliners (Kaiser Chiefs, the Prodigy) show that Coke Live can pull a few big names. Camping is also available.

September

6 (2009) **Dachshund Parade**
Barbican to Rynek Główny
Radio Krakow, 012 630 6000
Perhaps the city's most zany event is held in celebration of the Polish playwright Sławomir Mrożek, who asked

Dachshund Parade

for a parade of dachshunds when he arrived home in 1996. Subsequently, on the first Sunday in September, owners march their sausage dogs in all manner of costumes as they stroll down Floriańska to the main market square. A prize goes to the best-dressed hound.

13-19 (2009) **Sacrum Profanum**
Various locations
www.sacrumprofanum.pl
A week of modern classical and experimental music. See box p30.

October

21-25 (2009) **Unsound**
Various locations
www.unsound.pl
Unsound is a week-long festival of experimental and electronic music staged at interesting locations across town. 2008 saw performances by Michael Nyman and Ben Frost, the highlight being an eight-hour screening of Warhol's *Empire* to live music at the Galicia Jewish Museum.

Late Oct-early Nov
Zaduszki Jazz Festival
Various locations
www.deprofundis.glt.pl
Held for a week covering All Souls' Day, this long-established jazz fest brings name acts from Poland and abroad to venues across town.

November

Ongoing Zaduszki Jazz Festival (see October).

1-2 **All Souls' Day**
November 1 is a national holiday. Main Rakowicki Cemetery (p113) is halo'ed by mass candlelight.

3-7 (2009) **Joseph Conrad Literature Festival**
Various locations
www.conradfestival.pl
To be staged for the first time in 2009, this five-day event includes readings, seminars, lectures, concerts and theatrical pieces. Although this is not a

Conrad festival per se, the former Krakow schoolboy provides the inspiration for the theme of a literary world without borders. The Krakow Book Fair (www.targi.krakow.pl) follows.

8-15 (2009) **Festival of Polish Music**
Various locations
www.fmp.org.pl
Polish composers from the Middle Ages to the present day have works performed at the fifth annual FPM.

20-29 (2009) **Audio Art Festival**
Various locations
www.audio.art.pl
Krakow is one of six Polish cities to host this ten-day festival of experimental music, also webcast. Top acts to play in 2008 were François Houle from Vancouver and Loadbang Ensemble from Chicago.

27 Nov-4 Dec (2009) **Etiuda & Anima**
Various locations
www.etiudaandanima.com
The main independent film festival is divided into feature and animation categories and showcases works by international students.

December

Ongoing Etiuda & Anima (see November).

Dec **Christmas market**
Rynek Główny
www.krakow.pl
Traditional *szopka* nativity scenes are set up around the market square, backdropped by stalls of gifts and huts for mulled wine. A prize goes to the best *szopka*. Christmas itself is a family affair and little is open for business.

Dec 31 **New Year's Eve**
Rynek Główny
www.krakow.pl
Krakow's main market square is the setting for New Year merriment, with fireworks and music either side of the big countdown.

Itineraries

St Mary's Basilica

Rynek Główny

With the arguable exception of Brussels, no European city has a showcase medieval square as fine as Krakow's **Rynek Główny**. Certainly none has one as big, 200 metres by 200 metres. Its four sides, conveniently signposted A-B, C-D, E-F and G-H, can be swiftly walked in some 40 minutes.

But that would mean striding right past some of Krakow's most notable restaurants, grandest coffeehouses and finest landmark, **St Mary's Basilica**. There are also two branches of the **History Museum**, the **Town Hall Tower**, **St Adalbert's Church** and, centrepiecing the whole, the **Sukiennice Cloth Hall**. All in all, stopping off for drinks and a meal, a varied and satisfying half a day can be spent discovering Rynek Główny. Exploring it properly could take the intrepid visitor the best part of a week.

The square changes with the seasons. Summer sees open-air performances and full café terraces. Before Christmas, colourful nativity cribs, *szopka*, are displayed; Poland gathers here for New Year's Eve. Although traffic is light – buggies, horsedrawn carriages and pedalo vehicles for tourists – the market square always seems busy. After the nightlife babble dies down, after 2am, the hour is still marked by the bugler from atop St Mary's.

The city charter signed in 1257 after the Tartar invasion by Bolesław the Bashful, his mother Grzymisława and his wife Kinga declared that the settlement here should come under Magdeburg Law, calling for an orderly town centre to be built around a market square. Those familiar with classic (if mainly rebuilt) German cities, Prague or Brno could make an easy comparison upon arrival here.

function as a place of trade dates to the 1200s. A large plaque in the floor refers to 1257 and the Magdeburg Law – tourists brush past as you try to read it. Heraldic emblems from Poland's towns and provinces cover the white walls of the interior, filled with souvenir stalls. Facing out from beneath the colonnades are two cafés; landmark **Noworolski** was opened in 1910 and displays art-nouveau touches within. Of a sunny morning, it's a fine spot to start the day, breakfast enjoyed facing St Mary's Basilica.

The scaffolding alongside will be lifted in 2010 when a branch of the **National Museum** housing 19th-century Polish art reopens upstairs. Flanking the building are the statue of **Adam Mickiewicz**, Poland's national poet and a busy meeting point; and the Town Hall Tower, a free-standing remnant of the 14th-century town hall knocked down by the Austrians. In summer you can climb its 100 steps for a view of the city. At the foot is a plaque where Austria handed power over to Colonel Roja at the end of World War I – effectively granting Poland independence after 123 years.

Also at the base is a branch of the **Teatr Ludowy** ('People's Theatre') and the café-restaurant **Ratuszowa**, with outdoor seating. Nearby is the bronze head of *Eros Bendato*, on its side, sculpted by Igor Mitoraj, set up here in 2003. It complements Enrico Muscetra's *Suspended Dream*, a sculptural take on Romeo and Juliet, near the Cloth Hall's north-west corner.

You can start your outer walk nearby, at the right-angle of Szczepańska and Sławkowska, site of the **Golden Tiger** chemist dating back to 1814. This is the start of row A-B, Rynek Główny's northern flank, the shopfronts and coffeehouses catching the morning sun. Note the plaque signifying

Over 750 years, the square has witnessed many historic events – Tadeusz Kościuszko's rally against Russian rule in 1794, the official end of the Habsburgs in 1918 – but, miraculously, never has it been bombed or severely damaged. During the century when Poland was off the map, it was the keeper of Polish culture and language. After 1866, when Galicia received a certain autonomy from Vienna, Krakow became a quite free and creative hub. Many restaurants and cafés date from this period.

The grand façades, many neo-classical, owe their appearance to the Habsburg period. Their street numbers appear out of synch with the 1-47 order around the square. St Mary's (and the Hard Rock Café) are officially on adjoining plac Mariacki. Bank Pekao (one of many cashpoints) by Floriańska is No.47 but also carries a No.499 sign.

The prestigious address of Rynek Główny 1 belongs to the Cloth Hall. Its colonnaded arcades were added in the 1870s but its

ITINERARIES

Goethe's stay in 1790 and, further along by the **Redolfi** café, one marking the uprising of General Józef Chłopicki in 1831. Another call to arms, launched by Tadeusz Kościuszko in 1775, is marked a few doorways on. It's not all history – a tattoo parlour stands beside the Kurdish consulate.

You then arrive at Floriańska, the shopping street with even more amber boutiques than on the square. At this corner **Andrzej Kukla** juggles a football, the world-record holder pitching up with his dog, a sign of his achievements and a begging mat.

Time it right and you'll catch the unveiling of Veit Stoss' high altar at St Mary's at 11.45am, six days of the week. Buy a ticket from the office facing the visitors' entrance (Poles go in through the main door and pray at the back). Gathered with other tourists on the wooden benches, you see the altarpiece doors being opened by a nun with a long pole, to aptly grandiose music. It's an impressive sight, panels depicting scenes of the Assumption of the Virgin Mary. The altar stays open all day and the star-studded ceiling is always a crowd-pleaser.

The stretch from St Mary's to Grodzka takes in the square's main commercial hub, fashion stores flanking the upscale **Pasaż 13** centre. Halfway down this row, by the renowned **Szara** restaurant and café, is a plaque marking Poland's first post office, set up in 1558 and commemorated 400 years later. Szara itself is, like historic buildings here, a stone townhouse (*kamienica*) formed of two merged medieval houses. The history of ownership is given on a grey sign in English and Polish.

Grodzka marks where the Royal Route would have left the main square. Row E-F begins with the **Dom Polonii**, a hotel, restaurant

and shop where Chopin recitals are held. Three key spots then follow: restaurant **Wierzynek**; bookshop **Hetmańska**, another medieval conversion that housed the Royal Mint; and restaurant **Wentzl**, dated 1792. Facing them is **St Adalbert's**, peering over the pavement, lower than the square. While this diminutive church was being adapted in various styles (Gothic, Romanesque, Baroque), the square was built up around it.

Halfway along E-F is Bracka, the hub of bohemian Krakow in the dark old days. Today's cluster of bars and clubs (**Prowincja**, **Rdza**, Błędne Koło) don't have that hidden underground cachet but provide entertainment all the same.

After the sadly overlooked **International Cultural Centre**, a gallery and events space, the row ends at Wiślna. Here the **Galeria Centrum**, a shopping centre due for an upgrade after its purchase by Vistula menswear, faces a likeness of Bálint Balassi, the Hungarian poet who lived here in 1590.

This busy corner is best known for the activities in the **Pałac pod Baranami**, a mansion whose cellar housed a seminal cabaret. Student acts at Piotr Skrzynecki's **Piwnica pod Baranami** mocked the state, a risky business in the 1960s. Shows still run on Saturdays, while a jazz festival takes place here in July. A prominent cinema is housed in the same building, fronted by **Vis a Vis**, a real locals' bar whose poignant statue of Skrzynecki is always holding fresh flowers.

After Szewska, another bar hub, grand **Hawełka** and **Europejska** offer traditional dishes, alongside the **Krzysztofory Palace**, the central site of the **National Museum**, now under renovation. Its cellar hosted the Krakow Group, an influential collection of artists who met here either side of the war.

Jama Michalika

Modernist Krakow

The best start to any tour of
Modernist Krakow is to do
what the Modernists did: drink at
the **Jama Michalika** café (p60).
'Michalik's Den' on Floriańska still
echoes the era. Sober locals and
tourists comprise today's clientele
but the decor remains a riot of art-
nouveau wonders. Mad caricatures
leap out of corners, out-sized chairs
shoot up over their sitters' heads
and stained-glass unicorns sniff
cakes on silver platters. Poland's
first cabaret, the **Zielony Balonik**
('Green Balloon'), opened here in
1905. Puppets representing local
figures of the day recall what was
a decidedly adult kind of Punch
and Judy show. Stories of strange
goings-on did the rounds, of
devil worship and nude dancing.

Close to the Art Academy, the
café was the home from home of an
artistic community who came to be
known as **Młoda Polska**. The first

shocks of Modernism were
spreading across Europe and
Krakow's young were eager
to embrace the new dawn.

It was no coincidence that
Poland's Modernist movement
developed in Krakow. Close to
Vienna geographically and
politically, Krakow had received
a certain autonomy from southern
Poland's Habsburg masters; other
parts of the nation, wiped from the
map after Napoleon, had had their
identity smothered by the Prussian
or Russian authorities. Krakow
became Poland's spiritual capital.

Influential Polish families
brought their art collections to
Krakow, where a spirit of rebellion
and creativity thrived. Artists,
writers and creatives of every
stripe could question Austrian
rule and, by dint of their paintings,
literature and performances,
promote the notion of Poland.

Franciscan Church

Two decades after the movement was at its height, and ten years after the death of its key figure, the multi-talented Stanislaw Wyspiański (1869-1907), Poland got its independence. 'Movement' may be too grandiose a term, for Młoda Polska, 'Young Poland', was more of a loose community of bohemians, a scene, centred on the cabaret at the Jama Michalika. The scene was characterised by what it wasn't: bourgeois and romantic. It shunned the Positivists influenced by conservative historians. Młoda Polska wanted Poland for Poles.

Austrian officials, professors and old artists were all fair game at the Zielony Balonik. Participants mocked Krakow's pompous, provincial spirit and in the process created some of the most wondrous art that Poland has ever produced.

Those coming to Krakow to find something akin to Gaudí's Barcelona or Horta's Brussels will at first be disappointed. There isn't that much architecture to see. A more realistic comparison would be with Klimt's Vienna. Ten of the original 50 members of Klimt's anti-establishment movement, Sezession, were Poles. Many spent time in Paris – Wyspiański was an acquaintance of Gauguin. Art nouveau was Młoda Polska's signature art form. Its two main exponents, Wyspiański and Józef Mehoffer, studied under Jan Matejko at Krakow's Academy of Arts. Under a campaign to renew Krakow's monuments, each was commissioned to produce radical and striking works in stained glass for Krakow's historic churches.

The medieval **Franciscan Church** (p50) had been gutted by fire in 1850. Wyspiański was given carte blanche to cover the walls and vaults with murals, and produce one of his best-known works, the stained-glass kaleidoscopic blaze of colour showing God the Father creating the world. He also added stained-glass touches to **St Mary's Basilica** (p52).

The fiery images you see today connect with the personality of the artist who created them. An intense, ginger-bearded genius, Wyspiański was a painter, poet, playwright, designer of stage sets and stained-glass windows, as well as a creator of fantastical, if uncomfortable, furniture. His *Wesele* (*The Wedding*) practically invented modern Polish drama. Inspiration for the play came from a marriage party Wyspiański attended at Rydlowka (ulica Tetmajera 28, 012 637 0750), a peasant house just outside Krakow, which today is a **Młoda Polska Museum** of poetry, paintings and sundry documentation.

'Of all of Wyspiański's works, the most unusual was, without any doubt, himself,' recalled Tadeusz 'Boy' Zelenski, ringmaster of the Green Balloon cabaret. Considered too modern by many would-be patrons, the artist had several grand designs turned down. The Franciscan Church was where he managed to leave his mark. Near the church is the **Wyspiański 2000 Pavilion** (012 616 1886), designed by local architect Krzysztof Ingarden in 2007, a rare new building in the Old Town. The revolving bricks on the façade are emblazoned with chestnut leaves, symbols of Krakow during the Modernist era. (A whole staircase of chestnut leaves, another fanciful Wyspiański creation, can be seen at the **House of the Society of Physicians** at Radziwiłłowska 4.) Back in the pavilion, three windows made by artist Piotr Ostrowski are modern replicas of Wyspiański's designs for Wawel.

A detailed representation of what the artist called the Polish Acropolis, a remodelling of Wawel to reflect Polish history, can be viewed on the upper floor of the **Wyspiański Museum** (p54) on plac Szczepański, an essential stop on any Modernist tour. The former Szolajski House was converted for its current purpose in 2003. Sketches, drawings, set designs and foreign-language editions of *The Wedding* are on display, as well as black-and-white photographs of 19th-century Krakow. On the third floor are paintings, sculpture and furniture by Feliks 'Manggha' Jasieński, the great Japanese art collector and Wyspiański contemporary, plus puppets from the Zielony Balonik cabaret. A space for temporary exhibitions on the ground floor accommodates regular shows related to the Młoda Polska movement.

Flanking the western side of plac Szczepański is the graceful **Palace of Art** (p51), opened in 1901 and studded with busts of key fin-de-siècle figures. The nearby **Stary Theatre** (p74) displays a beautiful frieze from its art-nouveau make-over in 1905; downstairs the Maska café is another good spot for a coffee in Modernist surroundings.

Further west, just outside the Old Town, stands another Modernist landmark, the **Józef Mehoffer Museum** (p117). It's also the house where Mehoffer's great friend and contemporary Wyspiański was born. Mehoffer (1869-1946) did not die young but went on to become a respectable, moustachioed professor. The idea to convert the family home, bought in Mehoffer's later years, into a museum came from his son, Zbigniew. Not only does the house contain furnishings, interiors and original works (stained glass, oils, drawings) as Mehoffer would have left it but the lovely garden has been recreated as Mehoffer first designed. A café, the Ważka, serves full lunches and nice teas.

Both the Wyspiański Museum and Mehoffer House are branches of the **National Museum** (p120). Its main building stands a little further west, on a junction. The thrust of the 400-strong collection of paintings representing 20th-century Polish art is the Młoda Polska period. Here not only Wyspiański gets a dedicated room but also Olga Boznańska, whose *Girl with Chrysanthemums* is considered one of the classic works of the period. Wojciech Weiss, Józef Pankiewicz and Władysław Ślewiński also get a look-in. Still, you're bound to be drawn to the cartoons of monumental stained-glass works by Wyspiański (Wawel) and Mehoffer (Fribourg Cathedral, Switzerland).

ITINERARIES

1949 Club

Nowa Huta

Way out east, an easy journey from central Krakow by tram (Nos.4, 15 or 22), **Nowa Huta** is a different trip to Krakow. Whereas Krakow is bourgeois, cultured and characterised by grandiose churches, its unloved stepsister is a vast outpost of dystopian Socialism, grafted on to greater Krakow at Stalin's behest. When the recently installed Communist authorities voted on the best site for their workers' paradise, in May 1947, it was no coincidence that Krakow was chosen. Nowhere was the Church more powerful or the prevailing spirit more liberal. Joe personally arranged for an unrepayable loan to fund this massive operation: a new town of 200,000 people and, to keep them busy, a **Lenin Steelworks** complex so preposterously huge workers still need a network of buses to get around it.

The world's largest steel producer, India's Mittal, bought part of Nowa Huta in 2003 and increased its stake to 100 per cent in 2007. Today it employs fewer than 10,000 workers, less than a quarter than at its post-war peak.

But the rest of Nowa Huta – arrow-straight avenues, meticulously planned Socialist-Realist architecture and addresses arranged by district number and not street doors – are preserved exactly as planned in the late 1940s. There is even a new pride about the place. A (rather splendid) theme bar, **1949 Club**, sells 'I Love Nowa Huta' heart-sign T-shirts, a young entrepreneur makes a killing from Nowa Huta tours by Trabant (pay extra to visit a real apartment; www.crazyguides.com), and there's talk of installing a Museum of Communism in the Światowid Cinema. In 2008, Kraftwerk played

the steelworks for the Sacrum Profanum festival in keeping with its principle of staging music in industrial spaces.

In fact, apart from a statue of Lenin bought by eccentric Swedish millionaire Big Bengt Erlandsson for comedy value, the only slight Nowa Huta seems to have suffered post-1989 is the renaming of focal **plac Centralny** as Ronald Reagan Square. Everyone still refers to it by its old name. This is where to start your tour – whether you're coming by tram or Trabant.

From here you see Tadeusz Ptaszycki's Classicist geometry in the post-war street plan. Immediately ahead is **Aleja Róż**, lined with trees whose trunks are grey from pollution. At two o'clock is the renamed Aleja Solidarności, leading straight to the steelwork complex. This can only be visited by pre-arranged group visit but you get a feel of the place just from standing at the huge sign (now named after Polish engineer T Sendzimir) outside the main

entrance. The scale of the place is simply overwhelming. Workers here were among the most vocal to express their displeasure when the Solidarity movement rose against the authorities – subsequent Martial Law was brutal. Clashes were often violent, though locals could use their familiarity with Nowa Huta's confusing housing estates to hide quickly.

Just before Solidarity, Andrzej Wajda made his famous film *Man of Marble*, whose storyline (Nowa Huta bricklayer as anti-hero) and locations echo the zeitgeist.

Back on Róż, estates lurk behind the grand façades on either side. After dark, Nowa Huta can be quite edgy. Daytime, somewhere like the **Stylowa** (os Centrum 3) where Róż meets Al Przyjaźni, looking as it did when it first opened in 1956, is a friendly café to meet locals and get a feel for the place.

Further up Róż, past welcome greenery on the right-hand side, is the modest **Nowa Huta Tourist Information Centre** (os Słoneczne 16, 012 643 03 03; open 10am-2pm Tue-Sat), where staff are pleased to show you the **Nowa Huta History Museum** (012 425 97 75, www.mhk.pl/oddzialy/dzieje_nowej_huty; closed Mon, Sun; 5zł) in the same room. Exhibitions here are temporary and locally themed, usually involving posters or photographs from the post-war glory days.

Diagonally opposite stands a more ironic must-see, 1949 Club (os Urocze 12, 012 644 11 62, www.1949club.pl). Opened in 2006, this café is filled with old seats from the Sfinks cinema and classic black-and-white photographs from the same post-war era. Drawings of Nowa Huta buildings are for sale, as are T-shirts and splendid cakes.

A short walk up Róż and left down Mościckiego brings you to a Soviet tank, on the street outside the **Museum of the Armed Act** (os Górali 23, 012 644 35 17; open 10am-3pm Tue-Fri). Renovated in 2008, this Polish-only exhibition deals with sundry heroic actions undertaken by people from the area during World War II. Entry is free. Downstairs there's usually a social club of old locals playing cards or knitting and gossiping.

Ahead stands the landmark **People's Theatre** (os Teatralni 24, 012 680 21 12). Shows here often skirted controversy during political clampdowns. Its café is a handy place for a mid-tour snack.

Nearby, further up Obrońców Krzyża, stands the monument Nowa Huta is most proud of: the **Arka Pana Church** (No.1, 012 644 54 34). Authorities may rename squares and avenues but locals know that they themselves built this remarkable church brick by brick – the first laid by Karol Wojtyła (Pope John Paul II) himself in 1969. Eight years and millions of stones later, Wojciech Pietrzyk's ark-shaped construction was consecrated, a vast crucifix rising from its roof like a mast. Inside, the altar is of Carrara marble and the tabernacle contains crystal from the Moon, a gift from Apollo 11.

plac Centralny

Krakow by Area

Floriańska

Old Town

For quite some time, Krakow's **Old Town** *was* Poland. When maps showed only Prussia, Russia and Austria, after Napoleon and before World War I, the Stare Miasto and its centrepiece market square, **Rynek Główny**, kept the notion of Poland alive. Painters, writers, revolutionaries and architects thrived here in the late 1800s, the region granted enough autonomy from Vienna for Krakow to flower and bloom. The Austrians kept Krakow as grand as their own capital and just as orderly.

The result, untouched by Hitler or subsequent Socialism, is a pristine, postcard-perfect *centro storico* of grand townhouses, Baroque churches and neo-classical façades. True, today's Old Town is a prime shopping zone and filled with over 100 bars and restaurants.

But this oval of grid-patterned streets, circled by the green ring of Planty and abutted by the Polish Notre-Dame of Wawel, hasn't 'done a Prague'. You can find a burger bar and an internet café but you'll first see an *obwarzanki* bagel trolley and a coffeehouse terrace ideal for postcard writing. To walk the width of tram-free, (mainly) traffic-free Stare Miasto takes 15 minutes, the time needed to deal with a ticket machine, escalator and metro train in the Czech capital.

Time, therefore, to observe how hotels, banks and even shopping malls have been integrated into this kernel of civilised living, whose main sights – **St Mary's Basilica**, the **Town Hall Tower**, the market square itself – would be recognisable to Copernicus who studied round the corner.

North-south, from **Floriańska Gate** to **St Giles'**, runs the Royal Route. To the west is Copernicus' university quarter; just south is the ecclesiastical hub where Pope John Paul II resided. Key streets – **Św Jana**, **Floriańska**, **Grodzka** – can be crowded but never heaving.

Round the clock, on the hour, the bugler's four refrains from atop St Mary's remind pedestrians that the Old Town wasn't tainted by Turk or Tartar, Lancaster or Luftwaffe. Strolling between appointments, shops or late-night bars, it's always a timely and touching thought.

Sights & museums

Archdiocesan Museum

Kanonicza 19-21 (012 421 89 63/www. muzeumkra.diecezja.pl). **Open** 10am-4pm Tue-Fri; 10am-3pm Sat, Sun. **Admission** 5zł; 3zł reductions. **Map** p47 C5 ❶

The life and travels of locally born Pope John Paul II, Bishop of Krakow for 20 years, is illustrated here in painfully reverential detail. Diplomas, oil paintings, skis and a Pelikan kayak canoe point to the life of the orphan boy who kept goal for Cracovia and studied at the Jagiellonian University; skullcaps, a map and plane schedules of his Papal visits, and shelves of plates and salvers illustrate his activities post-1978. For all this, the interested visitor will know little more about Karol Wojtyła, the man; the casual visitor may not enjoy being followed round by a shuffling curator keen to amplify the legend in broken English.

Archaeology Museum

Senacka 3 (012 422 71 00/www.ma. krakow.pl). **Open** 9am-2pm Mon-Wed; 2-6pm Thur; 10am-2pm Fri, Sun. **Admission** 5zł; 3zł reductions. Free Sun. **Map** p47 B4 ❷

Impressive treasures from Ancient Egypt – sarcophagi, masks, mummified cats – haunt the dim, poorly documented rooms of this little-known museum. Set beside a lovely garden in a grand building used by the Austrians as a jail, the venue is crying out for a tourist-friendly overhaul. As it stands, the maps and models of the life of Stone-Age man in the Małopolska region mainly keep the mummies and museum attendants company.

Church of Sts Peter & Paul p49

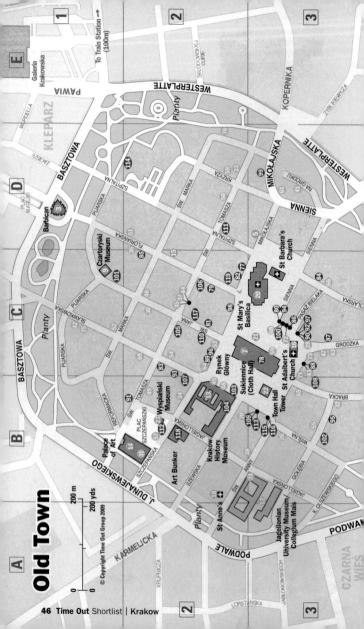

Old Town

To Train Station → (100m)

Galeria Krakowska

PAWIA

KLEPARZ

WESTERPLATTE

Planty

BASZTOWA

KOPERNIKA

WRZESZCZOWIE

WESTERPLATTE

SIENNA

Barbican **3**

Czartoryski Museum **9** **101**

FLORIAŃSKA

PIJARSKA

SW. MARKA

SZPITALNA

SZPITALNA

TOMASZA

MIKOŁAJSKA

St Barbara's Church

St Mary's Basilica **20** **77** **119**

106 **79**

Planty

Plac MATEJKI **3**

BASZTOWA

Planty

PIJARSKA

SŁAWKOWSKA

SW. MARKA

JANA

SW.

35 37 41
105 **117** **81**
110 **98**

Rynek Główny **7**

Sukiennice (Cloth Hall) **78**

St Adalbert's Church

Town Hall Tower

21

80 94
86
100 91 92 97
90 93
87
47 **53**
108 **85**
65

GRODZKA

BRACKA

WIŚLNA

GOŁĘBIA

SZEWSKA

PLAC SZCZEPAŃSKI

Wyspiański Museum **112**

Palace of Art **14**

Art Bunker

J. DUNAJEWSKIEGO

REFORMACKA

SW. TOMASZA

SW. JANA

91 **93** **107**
83
13
104 **103**
118

Krakow History Museum

70
109 **113**
115 **116**

55 **102**

St Anne's **18**

ANNY

Jagiellonian University Museum Collegium Maius

JAGIELLOŃSKA

KARMELICKA

KRUPNICZA

PODWALE

PLANTY

CZARNA WIEŚ

LORETAŃSKA

PODWA...

KOLETEK

0   200 m
0   200 yds

© Copyright Time Out Group 2009

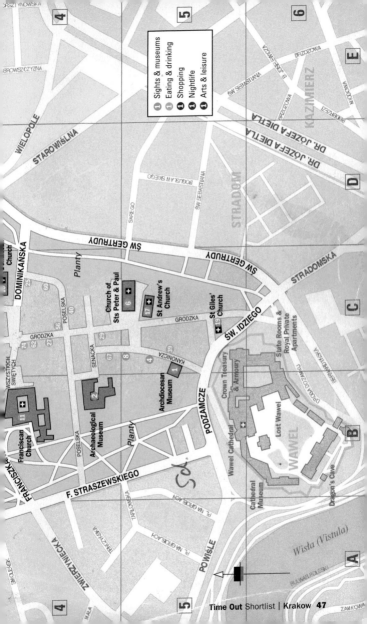

Legend
- 1 Sights & museums
- 1 Eating & drinking
- 1 Shopping
- 1 Nightlife
- 1 Arts & leisure

BROWSZCZYNA
JRSZLYNOWSKA

WIELOPOLE
STAROWIŚLNA

KAZIMIERZ

DR. JÓZEFA DIETLA

DR. JÓZEFA DIETLA

BRZOZOWA

SW. SEBASTIANA

STRADOM

SAPEGO
BOGUSŁAWSKIEGO
SW. SEBASTIANA

ŚW GERTRUDY

ŚW GERTRUDY

STRADOMSKA

DOMINIKAŃSKA

Planty

Church

Church of
Sts Peter & Paul

St Andrew's Church

St Giles' Church

ŚW. IDZIEGO

Suite Rooms &
Royal Private
Apartments

POSELSKA

GRODZKA

SENACKA

KRAKOWSKA

GRODZKA

Crown Treasury
& Armoury

PODZAMCZE

WISZYŃSKICH
ŚWIĘTYCH

Archaeological
Museum

Archdiocesan
Museum

Wawel Cathedral

Lost Wawel

WAWEL

Franciscan
Church

Planty

Cathedral
Museum

FRANCISZKAŃSKA

POSELSKA

F. STRASZEWSKIEGO

Dragon's Cave

PL NA GRÓB ACH

ZWIERZYNIECKA

TRYLOŃSKA

TRZECIESKA

PL NA GRÓBLACH

POWIŚLE

Wisła (Vistula)

BULWAR POLESKI

MAŁA

ZAŃKOWN

Barbican

Map p46 D1 ❸

Only put to good use in recent times, when exhibitions and classical music concerts are held here in June, this relic of medieval Krakow formed part of the city fortifications mainly demolished by the Austrians in the early 1800s. Its moat and drawbridge owe their stern appearance to fear of Turkish invasion – the grassed-over surface you see today makes for a pleasant entrance into the Old Town, via the connecting Floriańska Gate.

Bishop Erazm Ciołek Palace

NEW *Kanonicza 17 (012 429 15 58/ www.muzeum.krakow.pl).* **Open** 10am-6pm Tue-Sat; 10am-4pm Sun. **Admission** 20zł; 10zł reductions. *Old Polish Art* 12zł; 6zł reductions. *Orthodox Art* 6zł; 3zł reductions. Free Sun. **Map** p47 C5 ❹

With this grand reopening in late 2007, the National Museum is expanded by another venue, its collection of Polish art extended as far back as the 12th century. And the setting could not be more fitting: the beautiful palace of Bishop Erazm Ciołek, a major figure of late 15th-century Krakow. Two galleries comprise the museum, one of old Polish art (including pieces by Gothic craftsman Veit Stoss, of St Mary's fame); the other Orthodox art, bright Byzantine works from (mainly eastern) Poland and the Balkans.

Burgher House

Pl Mariacki 3 (012 422 42 19/www. mhk.pl). **Open** *Nov-Apr* 9am-4pm Wed, Fri-Sun; noon-7pm Thur. **Closed** 2nd Sun/mth. *May-Oct* 10am-5.30pm Wed-Sun. **Admission** 6zł; 4zł reductions. Free Wed. **Map** p46 D3 ❺

This most individual of the Krakow City Museums is a mock-up of how a well-to-do family lived in the 1600s, on the upper floor of a historic townhouse within bugle range of St Mary's. The family in question is the Hippolits, although some of the furniture, clocks and instruments belong to others from later eras. English documentation and

the personal feel of the effects – someone's fingers would have played this keyboard, someone's feet would have glowed beside the bedwarmer – make it a pleasant, worthwhile diversion.

Church of Sts Peter & Paul

Grodzka 38 (012 422 65 73). **Open** 9am-5pm Mon-Sat; 1-5pm Sun. **Admission** free. **Map** p47 C5 ❻

Created at the turn of the 16th and 17th centuries, this landmark on the Royal Route represents Baroque at its best. Its main features were all added later: the ornate tomb of Andrzej Trzebicki, followed by the high altar and the statues of the apostles lining the main railing facing Grodzka.

Cloth Hall

Rynek Główny. **Map** p46 C3 ❼

The centrepiece of the main market square will be clad in scaffolding until 2010, when the 19th-century branch of the National Museum reopens upstairs. Below, it's business as usual, tourists browsing the souvenir stalls between the colonnades, added in the 1870s to embellish this traditional place of trade since medieval times.

Cricoteka Museum

Kanonicza 5 (012 422 83 32). **Open** *Sept-June* 10am-4pm Mon-Fri. *July, Aug* 10am-4pm daily. **Admission** free. **Map** p47 C5 ❽

This former canon's house hosted the seminal Cricot-2 theatre company, founded by Tadeusz Kantor. The work of this influential dramatist and set designer is documented in written, video and costume form, invaluable for anyone keen to learn about Krakow's modern cultural development.

Czartoryski Museum

Św Jana 19 (012 422 55 66/www. muzeum-czartoryskich.krakow.pl). **Open** *Nov-Apr* 10am-3.30pm Tue, Thur, Sat, Sun; 10am-6pm Wed, Fri. *May-Oct* 10am-4pm Tue, Thur; 10am-7pm Wed, Fri, Sat; 10am-3pm Sun. **Admission** 10zł; 5z. reductions. Free Thur. **Map** p46 C1 ❾

KRAKOW BY AREA

Pharmacy Museum

This celebrated collection, treasures that changed hands between European royals, belonged to the noble Polish Czartoryskis. Pride of place goes to a rare Da Vinci oil painting, *Lady with an Ermine*. You'll also find Greek and Roman artefacts, plus weaponry and writings linked to 18th-century war and exploration. There's the odd Rembrandt too. A real treat over three floors, although detailed English documentation would be handy.

Dominican Church

Stolarska 12 (012 423 16 13). **Open** 8am-8pm daily. **Admission** free. **Map** p47 C4 ⑩

Although rebuilt in several architectural styles since its first stone was laid in 1250, this church off Grodzka is worth a look-in for its ornate chapels, most notably the Zbaraski to the left of the main entrance; and the Myszkowski and its impressive dome, by the pulpit.

Franciscan Church

Wyszstkich Świętych (012 422 53 76). **Open** 10am-4.30pm Mon-Fri; 1-4pm Sun. **Admission** free. **Map** p47 B4 ⑪

A key stop on any tour of Modernist Krakow, this 13th-century church suffered damage from fire and invasion before arriving at its current mix of Baroque, neo-Gothic and Stanisław Wyspiański's bright, sinuous forms of the early 1900s. His murals and stained-glass creations are best seen at sunset, when a golden light floods through the blues and yellows. See p37.

Jagiellonian University Museum/Collegium Maius

Jagiellońska 15 (012 422 05 49). **Open** *Oct-Mar* 10am-2.20pm Mon-Fri; 10am-1.20pm Sat. *Apr-Sept* 10am-2.20pm Mon, Wed, Fri; 10am-5.20pm Tue, Thur; 10am-1.20pm Sat. **Admission** *Tour* 12zł; 6zł reductions. Free *Apr-Sept* Tue. **Map** p46 A/B3 ⑫

This must-see is only accessible by guided tour, given in English at least twice a day, a swift and lively half-hour trot past priceless treasures in the field of science and astrology. Star of the show is old boy Nicolaus Copernicus, whose studies here in the 1490s led to his seminal work *De Revolutionibus*.

You'll see the globes and discs he used, although the documentation is not original – the later invading Swedes still keep it at Uppsala University. The guide usefully explains how the student's ecclesiastical know-how helped him avoid the wrath of the Church in publishing his revolutionary treatise. In the same narrow room is the first globe to depict the Americas, from the early 1500s, and the tour ends in the main Aula, scene of graduation ceremonies from NC's day to the present.

Krakow History Museum

Rynek Główny 35 (012 619 23 00/www. mhk.pl). **Open** 10am-5.30pm Wed-Sun. **Admission** 6zł; 4zł reductions. **Map** p46 B2 ⑬

During the renovation of the impressive Christopher's Palace housing an equally impressive collection of items relating to 700 years of city history, only temporary exhibitions are open to the public. Works continue until 2010. When it opens, museum highlights will include artefacts round under the main square during renovation.

Palace of Art

Pl Szczepański 4 (012 422 66 16). **Open** varies. **Admission** varies. **Map** p46 B2 ⑭

Hired out for temporary exhibitions and prestigious events, the Palace of Art is better known for the architectural detail embellishing its façade. Built by Franciszek Mączyński at the height of Modernism in 1901, it features busts of his renowned contemporaries (Matejko, Wyspiański) in expressions depicting the phases through which each artist must pass – despair, doubt, and so on. See p37.

Pharmacy Museum

Floriańska 25 (012 421 92 79). **Open** noon-6.30pm Tue; 10am-2.30pm Wed-Sun. **Admission** 6zł; 3zł reductions. **Map** p46 C2 ⑮

An absolute gem, this, a 15th-century building of five floors, three transformed to resemble an apothecary of a different era, with a laboratory in the cellar and a loft for drying herbs. The carefully created displays of (mainly) original jars, vessels and cases give the visitor an inkling of how locals lived way back when – would that other museums could do the same.

St Adalbert's Church

Rynek Główny (012 422 83 52). **Open** 9am-5pm Mon-Sat; 1.30-5pm Sun. **Admission** free. **Map** p46 C3 ⑯
The first thing you notice about this higgledy-piggledy anomaly right on the main square is that it's a few steps lower than everything else – evidence of how often the surroundings have been paved over since this was built 1,000 years ago. Built and rebuilt, in fact, for tiny though St Adalbert's is, it displays hints of Romanesque, Gothic and Baroque. Lower your head to enter and gawp at a few archaeological finds through the ages.

St Andrew's Church

Grodzka 56 (012 422 16 12). **Open** 7.30am-5pm daily. **Admission** free. **Map** p47 C5 ⑰
It may be the best part of 1,000 years old, and a fine example of Romanesque architecture, but St Andrew's wows visitors by its Baroque makeover by Baltasare Fontana in the early 18th century. Look out for the pulpit, built in the shape of St Peter's boat.

St Anne's Church

Św Anny 11 (012 422 53 18). **Open** 9am-noon, 4-7pm daily. **Admission** free. **Map** p46 B2 ⑱
The Baroque influence of Baltasare Fontana can be seen all over this originally Gothic church, frequented by alumni of the nearby Jagiellonian University (including Copernicus). The ornate shrine you'll see on the right-hand side from the main entrance is of St John of Kęty, a professor shortly before the Copernicus era.

St Giles' Church

Św Idziego 1 (no phone). **Open** *for services* daily. **Admission** free. **Map** p47 C5 ⑲
Just below Wawel on the Old Town side, this 1,000-year-old church is used for concerts in summer and mass in English every Sunday morning. It's

another patchwork of architectural styles but its most striking feature is outside: the memorial cross to Katyń, erected 50 years after the notorious atrocity committed by Soviet forces on Polish officers – and erected only months after guilt was acknowledged by Gorbachev in 1990.

St Mary's Basilica

Pl Mariacki 5 (012 422 05 21). **Open** 11.30am-6pm Mon-Sat; 2-6pm Sun. *Altar opening* 11.50am-6pm Mon-Sat. **Admission** 6zł; 3zł reductions. **Map** p46 C3 ⑳
One of the wonders of the Gothic world is this twin-towered marvel dominating the north-east corner of the main square. Beneath a star-studded ceiling in a sky-blue firmament, Veit Stoss' celebrated high altar occupies the wall by the visitors' entrance. Further back, only Poles can go through the main entrance to whisper prayers or use the confession box. Tourists flock here at 11.45am six days a week, to witness the shutters being opened (by a nun wielding a long pole, to grandiose music) of Stoss' 12-metre-high masterpiece. Some of the faces on the colourful, detailed panels depicting the Assumption of the Virgin Mary are said to be modelled on real ones Stoss would have met. Afterwards (although the altar stays open all day), visitors emerge to glimpse the bugler waving to them from the window of the tallest tower, after giving his ritual hourly four blasts from each of its corners.

Statue of Adam Mickiewicz

Rynek Główny. **Map** p46 C3 ㉑
Everyone's favourite meeting place is this grand landmark in the main square, circled by marble benches. The figure, Poland's national poet, spent much of his life in exile, only coming to Krakow for burial at Wawel.

Town Hall Tower

Rynek Główny 1 (012 619 23 20). **Open** *May-Oct* 10.30am-2pm, 2.30-5pm daily. **Admission** 5zł; 3.50zł reductions. **Map** p46 C3 ㉒

Lightly does it

Ancora sets culinary standards for Krakow to follow.

'We didn't want to compete with traditional places in the Old Town,' began Adam Chrząłowski, explaining his roundabout journey to running Krakow's finest contemporary restaurant, **Ancora**. 'Farmers' cooking, pork chops and everything, just wasn't for us.'

Krakow's top chef has limited experience of *pierogi* dumplings and *bigos* stew anyway. As a philosophy student in Warsaw, Adam worked in kitchens to fund foreign study. In Zürich, he spent six months at a restaurant. 'That's when I fell in love with cooking,' said Adam. 'Up until then, it was just a means to an end.'

After moving back to Warsaw, he worked in the kitchens of the five-star Sheraton and Bristol hotels.

'Polish gastronomy was killed in the 40 years after the war,' he says. 'It was only about filling people up, not dining. Only when I worked in top-class hotels did I realise what international standards were.'

After a two-year stint as a chef in Shanghai, Adam worked with Kurt Scheller at Warsaw's prestigious Rialto -- his last 'apprenticeship'.

'It was always my dream to run my own place,' he continues, 'and Krakow made more sense. Warsaw is for business. Here visitors and locals can enjoy food. And everything is concentrated in the Old Town – everybody knows where to go.'

If they want *pierogi* and *bigos*, that is. In 2007, Adam broke the mould with Ancora (see p54). 'Poland has great game, forest fruits and river fish but cooking techniques hadn't changed since the war,' he says. 'I wanted to use our quality products as a base for a lighter, modern cuisine.'

New technique allows Adam to make his meats more tender, his mushrooms more succulent, and his seasonal sauces and dressings more varied. Along with a high-standard oven in the open kitchen, Adam and his small team created a simple venue, no frills or tablecloths, the wall of filled racks hinting at the selection of more than 400 wines.

Duck breast and suckling pigs are currently sourced from Germany, the rest locally. Polish suppliers, like Krakow's chefs, are having to raise their standards fast to keep up with Adam's runaway success.

Café Philo p57

Get the best view of the Old Town from this 14th-century remnant of the original town hall, open in summer for those willing to scale its 100 steps. You can see how the town hall looked in scale-model form in a display near the foot of the tower, where a plaque also marks the declaration of Polish independence here in 1918.

Wyspiański Museum

Ul Szczepańska 11 (012 422 70 21).
Open *Oct-Apr* 11am-6pm Tue-Fri;
10am-3.30pm Sat, Sun. *May-Sept* 10am-6pm Tue-Fri; 10am-3.30pm Sat, Sun.
Admission 8zł; 4zł reductions. Free Sun. **Map** p46 B2 ㉓

This entertaining and comprehensive overview of the most famous figure of the Modernist era illustrates the work of this playwright, architect and art-nouveau artist in book, model and painting form. See p37.

Eating & drinking

A1

NEW *Św Anny 6 (012 429 50 12/www.
a1restauracja.com.pl).* **Open** noon-midnight daily. **Bar-restaurant.**
Map p46 B3 ㉔

The recently opened A1, lilac-tinted within, sun-tinted terrace without, brings a contemporary touch to the staid academic quarter. On offer are 'steak, sushi and cocktails', plus continental and Asian mainstays, of a range and standard suitable for most impressionable would-be lovers. The clincher is the bill – presented in a dinky sea-shell case lined with rose petals.

Ancora

*Dominkańska 3 (012 357 33 55/
www.ancora-restaurant.com).*
Open noon-11pm daily. **Restaurant.**
Map p47 C4 ㉕

Imaginative, contemporary dishes by Adam Chrząstowski. See box p53.

Aqua e Vino

*Wiślna 5-10 (012 421 25 67/www.
aquaevino.pl).* **Open** noon-11pm daily.
Bar-restaurant. Map p47 B3 ㉖

Part lounge bar, part chic eatery, one of the most reputable Italians dots its menu with the odd dish and drink from the Veneto: hearty soups and game; a zingy sgroppino dessert of sparkling wine, vodka and lemon sorbet.

Balaton

Grodzka 37 (012 422 04 69). **Open** noon-10pm daily. **Restaurant. Map** p47 C4 ㉗

For all the positives of Krakow's culinary gentrification, it is comforting to know that this old-school Hungarian restaurant can still fill its two-room space of dark wood and rustic trimmings. Equally comforting and filling here are the breaded meats, soups and game stews, served by waistcoated waiters straight out of central casting.

Bar 13

Pasaż 13, Rynek Główny 13 (012 617 02 12). **Open** 9am-9pm Mon-Sat; noon-5pm Sun. **Café-bar. Map** p46 C3 ㉘

As smart as its stablemate wine boutique and delicatessen in the lower-ground floor of chic commercial hub Pasaż 13, Bar 13 offers Italian cheeses by the platter, decent Chianti and pinot grigio by the glass, quality cakes and limoncello to a non-smoking professional crowd sat at half-a-dozen tables.

Bar Grodzki

Grodzka 47 (012 422 68 07). **Open** 9am-9pm Mon-Sat; 10am-7pm Sun. **Restaurant. Map** p47 C4 ㉙

Daytime opening immediately after breakfast, tiled interior, traditional chintz, set varieties of pancake and *pierogi* – with no price tag over 15zł – the Grodzki is Krakow at its most authentically retro, pleasing to pensioner and Interrailer alike.

Baroque

NEW *Św Jana 16 (012 422 01 06/ www.baroque.com.pl).* **Open** 11am-midnight daily. **Bar-restaurant. Map** p46 C2 ㉚

Fashion TV plays beside images of foxy, masked figures, while a moneyed clientele peruses a menu of 150-plus vodkas (Tatra, Cracovia, Sobieski Cranberry, every Wyborowa under the sun); cocktails mixed with fresh fruit and sundry syrups, and main dishes such as tempura or beefsteak. Does a handy line in outside catering too.

Bunkier Café

Pl Szczepański 3A (012 431 05 85). **Open** 9am-2am daily. **Café. Map** p46 B2 ㉛

Perfect place to plot up on the Planty green ring, the equally verdant Bunkier is quietly busy with coffee-sippers from breakfast past bedtime, all year round. Umbrella heaters warm winter drinkers. More intimate seats can be found in the arty gallery space above.

Café Botanica

Bracka 9 (012 422 89 80/www. cafebotanica.pl). **Open** 8.30am-midnight daily. **Café. Map** p46 B3 ㉜

Cherubino p58

Part garden, part café, the Botanica is literally overflowing with greenery. Equally abundant is the fare on offer: Brazilian and Ethiopian coffees; wines from Bordeaux and Beaujolais; flans of salmon and cheese; tortellini of several fillings; and a teetering cake display by the prime seats in the window.

Café Philo

Św Tomasza 30 (mobile 0513 06 79 96). **Open** 8am-late daily. **Bar**. **Map** p46 D2 ③③
Chain-smoking students yak or gaze into space amid groaning bookshelves and classic scenes of Paris. It all sounds a tad pretentious but this is dedicated escapism – Café Philo used to operate 24 hours, as did its regulars.

Café Zaćmienie

Ul Szczepańska 3 (012 431 08 64). **Open** 9am-1am Mon-Fri, Sun; 9am-2am Sat. **Café**. **Map** p46 B2 ③④
Hiding a secret garden in a downtown location, on the other side of a dinky bridge from an inner courtyard, the dim 'Café Eclipse' offers relaxation and dark Warka beer. The swing seat for two outside was just made for lovers.

Camelot

Św Tomasza 17 (012 421 01 23). **Open** 9am-midnight daily. **Café**. **Map** p46 C2 ③⑤
Bookending a busy right-angle of bars and restaurants by St John's Church, Camelot comprises three candlelit rooms, one with a chandelier, in which breakfasts, fresh juices and superior drinks and snacks are served. These include mountain-style *żurek* soup, hot raspberry wine, rose liqueur and sundry boozy-fruity concoctions. Infrequent shows are given downstairs – above are a gallery and bookshop.

Carlito

Floriańska 28 (012 429 19 12). **Open** 10am-midnight daily. **Restaurant**. **Map** p46 D2 ③⑥
By no means the best pizzeria in town but perhaps the most convivial, given its roof terrace overlooking Floriańska. Ten choices of pizza come in two sizes; saffron, rosemary and chanterelle mushrooms are put to good use in the ten pastas. There are grilled meat dishes too, plus salmon with grapefruit, and mussels in mild or spicy sauces.

Cyrano De Bergerac p59

Nic Nowego p63

Cherubino

*Św Tomasza 15 (012 429 00 07/www.
cherubino.pl).* **Open** noon-midnight
Mon-Sat; noon-11pm Sun. **Restaurant**.
Map p46 C2 ㊲

With tasty Italian touches to the menu
(spicy spaghetti with garlic, olive oil
and peperoncino), rustic Polish touches to the decor (including the carriages
that transported beer from this former
bottling plant), Cherubino is convenient for a decently priced dinner.

Chimera

*Św Anny 3 (012 423 21 78/www.
chimera.com.pl).* **Open** noon-midnight
daily. **Restaurant**. **Map** p46 B2/3 ㊳

Traditional Polish cuisine of this quality is not so hard to come by these days
but the Chimera can offer pedigree in
spades. Professors from nearby insti-
tutions and wealthier tourists tuck into
goose breast in honey with plums and
apricots in surroundings that exude the
19th-century origins of the dishes on
offer. There's an extensive salad bar,
probably the best in town, a garden in
summer and theatre shows for kids
every Sunday at noon.

Copernicus

*Copernicus Hotel, Kanonicza 16 (012
424 34 21).* **Open** noon-midnight
daily. **Restaurant**. **Map** p47 C5 ㊴

The most prestigious of the city's hotel
restaurants is this Relais & Châteaux
one in the Likus group. Presidents and
Oscar-winning directors sit beneath a
Renaissance ceiling while being served
dishes such as venison with roasted
foie gras from a seasonally changing
menu. If you fancy splashing out, come
in summer when the roof terrace opens.

Corleone

Poselska 19 (012 429 51 26). **Open**
noon-11pm daily. **Restaurant**. **Map**
p47 C4 ㊵

Comfortable and friendly Italian just
off the main sightseeing drag attracts
a healthy number of tourists. Look out
for the daily menu at 24zł and hefty
mains like chops or steak.

Cul-De-Sac

*Hotel Gródek, Na Gródzku 4 (012 431
90 30/www.donimirski.com).* **Open**
noon-11pm daily. **Restaurant**. **Map**
p46 D3 ㊶

Chef Rafał Targosz provides consistently fine fare in the airy lower-ground floor of the historic Gródek. Making deft use of seasonal ingredients, herbs and spices to complement veal, marlin, scallops and other delicacies, Targosz offers a 20-strong menu (starters and mains) of imagination and variety. Soups on this visit included ginger bouillon with macaroni, crayfish with steamed leeks and cream of courgette with ricotta cheese dumplings. For the quality, prices are perfectly reasonable.

Cyrano De Bergerac

Sławkowska 26 (012 411 72 88). **Open** noon-midnight daily. **Restaurant.** Map p46 C1 ㊷

Anna Nowak-Rivière renovated this former lodging for medieval tradesmen and 19th-century mead cellar in the 1990s, furnishing the two-storey space with fine tapestries and antiques, creating a cigar bar at street level. The French-oriented menu is as good as you'll find in town – the deer medallions with cranberry sauce usually ensure a return visit, budget willing.

Da Pietro

Rynek Główny 17 (012 422 32 79). **Open** 12.30-11.30pm daily. **Restaurant.** Map p46 C3 ㊸

Acknowledged to do the best steaks in town, this labyrinthine basement Italian on the market is named after cabaret star Piotr Skrzynecki, who opened the venue in 1992. Considering the setting and the standard (perhaps duck in honey-and-lemon sauce with figs next time?), prices are fair.

Dym

Św Tomasza 13 (012 429 66 61). **Open** 10am-midnight daily. **Bar.** Map p46 C2 ㊹

Barflies cluster around 'Smoke' like moths to a flame, propping up the zinc bar counter, or taking a table in the chatty front space or more private mezzanine. Everyone seems to know each other but that won't stop you pulling up a barstool and feeling involved.

Europejska

Rynek Główny 35 (012 429 34 93). **Open** 8am-midnight daily. **Café.** Map p46 B2 ㊺

Vintage coffeehouse beside Hawełka on the main square, whose bizarre retro British touches – red phone box, ads for Black & White whisky – offset a classic Central-European appearance. And it's not only coffee and cakes, far from it – there's a huge list of teas and wines, five types of breakfast (including bacon and eggs), mains such as duck breast in blackcurrant sauce, and Belvedere vodka in the cocktails.

Farina

Św Marka 16 (012 422 16 80/www. farina.krakow.pl). **Open** noon-midnight daily. **Restaurant.** Map p46 C2 ㊻

Chef Monika Turasiewicz runs a tidy ship here at Krakow's most renowned establishment for fish and seafood. Comfortably modern, Farina receives fresh supplies of mussels, oysters and other fruits de mer from Brittany and Italy Thursdays to Sundays. An extensive menu also offers dover sole, sea bass and other whole fish baked in herbs and garlic. Home-made pastas are another speciality – there's a black variety to accompany octopus and mussels – and the numerous choices for kids are a nice and handy touch.

Gruzińskie Chaczapuri

Grodzka 3 (012 432 26 00). **Open** 11am-midnight daily. **Restaurant. Map** p46 C3 ㊼

This won't be the best Georgian you've ever tasted but for visiting vegetarians, it's a boon. This red-fronted chain of four spots in the Old Town plus branches in Warsaw and Wrocław has made a success out of sundry stews and sauces of aubergine, tomato and pepper, though the meats are rather bland and disappointing. A number of Georgian wines run from a humble glass of Tblisuri to a bottle of ruby Kvanchkara – the beer is Polish-only.

Hawełka

Rynek Główny 34 (012 422 06 31). **Open** 11am-11pm daily. **Café-restaurant. Map** p46 B2 ㊽

The date of 1876 is something of a red herring – Antoni Hawełka's grocery Pod Palmą only became a restaurant in 1913 – but this landmark diner and coffeehouse exudes Habsburg elegance. Specialities include pork knuckle, a salad of duck breast and bilberry, and soups of porcini mushroom. You could also spend a sunny half-hour on the terrace with a coconut cake in poppy-and-raspberry sauce, but do take a gander at Włodzimierz Tetmajer's fine murals inside before you go.

Huśtawka

Św Tomasza 9 (no phone). **Open** 9am-midnight daily. **Bar. Map** p46 B2 ㊾

'Swing' swings – it also smokes and falls into chatter as light-hearted as the 18th-century French characters reproduced across one wall. The rest of the two-room space is quite jazzy, a deliberate mess of scuffed floorboards, mismatching furniture and framed violins.

Ipanema

Św Tomasza 28 (012 422 53 23). **Open** noon-midnight daily. **Restaurant. Map** p46 D2 ㊿

Colourful and unpretentious, this Brazilian diner sticks to its task of providing fill-ups (avocado soup, meats with black beans or in coconut sauce) from South America – there's *feijoada* for up to three people. Prices reflect the location rather than kitchen creativity but a dozen varieties of cachaça-based drinks give your visit a little zing.

Jama Michalika

Floriańska 45 (012 422 15 61). **Open** 9am-10pm Mon-Sat. **Café. Map** p46 D2 (51)

Forever associated with its heyday as a hangout for the leading members of the Młoda Polska movement at the turn of the last century, this historic coffeehouse of dark wood and green furnishings respects its legend. The back room where the seminal Zielony Balonik cabaret was staged exudes grandeur, accentuated by the selection of traditional honey-based tipples and dishes like quail in cranberry sauce. See p37.

Kuchnia Staropolska – 'U Babci Maliny'

Sławkowska 17 (012 422 76 01). **Open** 11am-8pm Mon-Sat; noon-8pm Sun. **Restaurant. Map** p46 C1 (52)

The most celebrated of Krakow's cheap, daytime eateries remains defiantly old-school – you may be a tourist on a budget but you'll pay the 1zł charge to use the toilet the same as everyone else. Wood features heavily, furniture, occasionally plates and cutlery, as does meat for the mains and mushrooms in many soups. Portions are Mr Creosote-sized. You won't be able to eat until next Tuesday without medical assistance. Self-service only.

Loža

Rynek Główny 41 (012 429 29 62). **Open** 9am-midnight daily. **Café-restaurant. Map** p46 C2 (53)

Prominent and popular with locals of a certain age, this two-floor operation comprises a cream-coloured, arty café at street level, and a restaurant below. Prices reflect the location and perceived role as a cultural landmark. Posters for theatre shows line the walls

Wiśniowy Sad p67

of the 'Actors' Club' upstairs, where delicious ice-cream desserts and cocktails mixed with Żubrówka vodka are served. You'll pay a pretty penny for duck in cranberry and apple or chicken shashlik in truffle sauce downstairs.

Metropolitan

Sławkowska 3 (012 421 98 03). **Open** 7am-11pm daily. **Café-restaurant.** **Map** p46 C2 ⑤④

Krakow's best choice for breakfast is also a decent spot for cosmopolitan dining all day thanks to the contemporary, global touch of South African chef Des Davies. Treat your hangover to grilled delights or take the kids for pancakes and syrup. The modern, wooden interior also suits a working lunch of the Met club sandwich (with turkey breast and crispy bacon) or a longer dinner of creole shrimp pasta.

Migrena

Gołębie 3 (012 430 24 18). **Open** 9am-11pm daily. **Bar**. **Map** p46 B3 ⑤⑤

Alongside a nameless bar similar in (small) size and (bohemian) nature, and

diagonally opposite the popular Cztery Pokoje, Migrena is both convenient and convivial. Photographs of India and a dinky replica of Krakow's skyline provide decor. Many come here to start the night and never leave.

Miód Malina

Grodzka 40 (012 430 04 11/www. miodmalina.pl). **Open** noon-11pm Mon-Fri; 11am-11pm Sat, Sun. **Restaurant.** **Map** p47 C4 ⑤⑥

The best choice for that homely Polish gastronomic treat – always book a table, people get turned away on cold nights in January. However busy it gets, you won't wait long to order from the long menu – the staff at the Honey Raspberry are kind and efficient. The kitchen has an equally delicate touch: the plum sauce and honey to accompany the spare ribs, the cranberry and horseradish to go with the beef tenderloin steak. Save room for dessert, warmed (vanilla caramel sauce on apple pancake) where necessary. The management has recently branched out with Wesele on the main square.

Zapiecek Polskie Pierogarnie p67

Morskie Oko

Pl Szczepańska 8 (012 431 24 23).
Open noon-11pm daily. **Restaurant**.
Map p46 B2 ⓗ

Although it's on Krakow's doorstep, hilly Zakopane doesn't get much of a culinary look-in here. This rustic restaurant, named after the lake in the Tatras, fills the gap. Bring an appetite – the waiter in regional garb plonks hefty dishes on to your sturdy wooden table: perhaps a fried sheep's cheese starter, barley soup, then a main of highlander-style potato pancakes. Fiddlers get going on busy nights.

Nic Nowego

Św Krzyża 15 (012 421 61 88). **Open** 7am-midnight Mon-Thur, Sun; 10am-11am Fri, Sat. **Pub**. **Map** p46 D2 ⓘ

'Nothing New' is ironic, for Tom Naughton's sleek venue is anything but the standard craic-by-rote Irish pub found all over Europe. Here decor, drinks and attitude are pleasingly contemporary. Naughton's experienced touch in the kitchen comes in handy too – you won't find better pub grub in Poland. You will find Guinness and Sky Sports, though – hence the crush three-deep in the narrow bar area.

Noworolski

Rynek Główny 1-3 (012 422 47 71). **Open** 9am-midnight daily. **Café**. **Map** p46 C3 ⓙ

As prominent and as landmark as it gets, this historic coffeehouse sits between the colonnades of the Cloth Hall luxuriating in the prestigious address of 'Rynek Główny 1-3'. Opened in 1910, hence the lovely art-nouveau interior, Noworolski has attracted Lenin, sundry major-league Nazis and, since the early 1990s, every tourist in town, thanks to a spruce-up and a prime spot facing St Mary's. Mains like pork sirloin in pepper sauce can be ordered, but most opt for a naughty dessert (banana in coconut dough, pancake with apple) and a long gawp.

Paese

*Poselska 24 (012 421 62 73/www.
paese.com.pl).* **Open** 1-11pm daily.
Restaurant. **Map** p47 C4 ⓚ

Radical, chic – and Polish

Punkt puts the punk into Krakow fashion.

From her location in the Old Town, award-winning artist/designer Monika Drożyńska has created some of the most original and daring clothes and accessories in Poland. **Punkt**, Drożyńska's brand, has its outlet on ulica Slawkowska (see p70). The items Monika creates, often re-creates, are more than just unusual – they open a debate about the very activity of buying clothes. 'Currently, I am working on a skirt as if designed by moths, with large holes in it. In summer, I shall relaunch Disappearing Earrings – they are made of ice and meant to cool and slowly vanish in the heat.'

Only an artist could conceive such inventions. Born in southern Poland in 1979, Monika graduated from the Jan Matejko Academy of Fine Arts in Krakow. 'I'm self-taught in fashion design,' she says. 'During my studies I started designing and sewing clothes for myself. Afterwards I started working for a fashion designer but there was no me in it. I decided to start my own brand with my friend, to feel free in my work.'

The friend was Maja, a graduate in cinematography. In the States, the girls had seen exclusive vintage fashion, and liked it. Creating items out of curtains and bedspreads – shower curtains, train compartment upholstery, anything was fair game – the pair sold items in central Krakow. In 2004, they launched Punkt.

'The local fashion scene was tiny and not diversified,' explains Monika. 'I was looking for fun in art, fashion and Polish folk traditions. We wanted our clothes to be comfortably functional, something almost to be worn as a second skin.'

Punkt caught on. In 2008, the British Council named Monika 'International Young Fashion Entrepreneur'. Monika, ever the radical, has contributed to Krakow's traditional nativity scene competition with a tumour in formaldehyde. Another project, 'Łódź-boat', involved her building a boat on her roof.

'Undoubtedly, Punkt has made a difference,' she reckons. 'I am launching two to four new projects every month. My favourite is to sell scarves by the metre – the length is up to the customer.'

'Ultimately,' concludes Monika, 'we have no business plan as such, but our intention is to get across the idea of Punkt to potential customers abroad.'

Poland's only Corsican restaurant leans heavily on Provençal dishes to offer diners in its four rooms ample choice, but it's a decent evening out for all that. Seasonal vegetables are used where possible, the meat and shellfish are generally reliable and the sorbets (strawberry and cognac, blackcurrant, apple and cinnamon) are a real delight.

Paparazzi

Mikołajska 9 (012 429 45 97). **Open** 11am-1am Mon-Fri; 4pm-1am Sat, Sun. **Bar. Map** p46 D3 ⓺⓵

Now a chain across Poland, this smart and savvy cocktail bar still feels somewhere special – the Sopot Sling with Wyborowa pear or Polmos Cooler with Żubrówka are not available in Warsaw, for example. Chatty staff know their mixes – it's fancy but not snobby. Food includes curries, pastas and burgers. No stag parties, please.

Pod Aniołami

Grodzka 35 (012 421 39 99/www. podaniolami.pl). **Open** 1-11pm daily. **Restaurant. Map** p47 C4 ⓺⓶

Using some of its recipes from a royal cookbook dating back to 1682, 'Under the Angels' is aptly set in a grand townhouse built shortly afterwards. Choose a spot in the Gothic cellar or, in summer, a garden in the stately courtyard. Dishes exude equal grandeur: nobleman's shashlik of pork roasted in wine with prunes and roasted apple, for example. Some seriously hearty choices must be ordered days in advance, such as the whole baked young boar. All is prepared within sight of your table and brought by an efficient waitstaff commendably spared the ignominy of wearing historical garb. Worth the hefty outlay.

Pod Gwiazdami

Hotel Rezydent, Grodzka 5 (012 430 26 57). **Open** noon-10pm daily. **Restaurant. Map** p46 C3 ⓺⓷

Modestly priced, close to the main square and often half-empty, 'Under the Stars' should be more patronised than its many nearby competitors. Here you're treated to a choice of tables,

plus local and house specialities such as the starters of herring or *maczanka* pork slices, both Krakow-style; and mains of pork knuckle in beer sauce and spicy horseradish. Traditional side dishes include hot, fried sauerkraut, tomatoes in garlic sauce and hot beetroot. All is aptly backdropped by images of the city in its sepia days.

Pod Winogronami

Hotel Pałac Bonerowski, Św Jana 1 (012 374 13 10). **Open** 5-11pm daily. **Restaurant. Map** p46 C2 ⓺⓸

One of Krakow's top hotel restaurants divides its cuisine into French and Italian elements, so its moneyed clientele can choose the Châteaubriand with duck foie gras over the beef sirloin tagliatta with rucola salad and parmesan. Among the many thoughtful touches are the raspberry vinaigrette to accompany the oysters, and the peperoni pepper sauce to complement the frogs' legs, classy starters both. The setting, overlooking the main square, couldn't be better.

Prowincja

Bracka 3-5 (no phone). **Open** 8am-11pm daily. **Café. Map** p46 B3 ⓺⓹

Back in the day, this lived-in stretch of Bracka by the main square attracted what passed for bohemians and marginals. This ramshackle two-floor café echoes that atmosphere, a place where you can relax over a Vergnano coffee or celebrated hot chocolate, or a fruity shot of some kind. The scuffed chairs outside get snapped up on warm evenings. Next door's Nowa Prowincja is, as its name suggests, more modern.

Siesta

Stolarska 6 (012 431 14 88). **Open** 9am-midnight Mon-Fri; 11am-midnight Sat, Sun. **Café. Map** p46 C3 ⓺⓺

By the Mały Rynek, this pleasant, arty, cig-free café can provide hot, spicy wine (or beer) on a winter's eve, alcoholic ice-cream desserts on a summer's afternoon, and its house coffee (with chocolate or caramel sauce) every morning. Handy hideaway for a romantic liaison between non-smokers.

Smak Ukraiński

Kanonicza 15 (012 421 92 94).
Open noon-10pm daily. **Restaurant**.
Map p47 C4 ⑥⑦

This quiet, smoke-free, two-room stone cellar operates as a Ukrainian eaterie, rustic and modestly priced, serving soups and salads similar to their Polish counterparts (beetroot, pork and sauerkraut) and wines from across the former Soviet Union (Moldova, Crimea, Georgia). Look out for the non-alcoholic bread beer *kvas*, and a dish from Lvov, pork with plums and apple sauce.

Szara

Rynek Główny 6 (012 421 66 69).
Open 11am-11pm daily. **Restaurant**.
Map p46 C3 ⑥⑧

Set in a grand historic townhouse on the main market square, 'Grey' is one of the city's landmark restaurants. Cream soup of porcini mushrooms, veal rolls braised in port wine, Szara salad with marinated salmon, avocado and shrimp – discerning diners are treated to the full gamut of local and house favourites in historic, vaulted surroundings. The adjoining bar is a rare and welcome contemporary drinkerie looking out over the square, offering mojito cocktails and a wide choice of wine.

Vinoteka La Bodega

Sławkowska 12 (012 425 49 81).
Open 10am-11pm daily. **Wine bar-restaurant**. **Map** p46 C2 ⑥⑨

A well chosen selection of Spanish wines matches a carefully conceived mix of *pintxos* and platters at this rather smart bodega and boutique. Buy your bottles at the back – the front area and pavement tables are for grazing on Serrano ham and Spanish cheeses over a glass of Arzuaga Crianza. A larger appetite should be satisfied with grilled bacon and prunes, or even a steak. A *cortado* should follow, a small measure of strong coffee with a dash of milk.

Vis a Vis

Rynek Główny 29 (012 422 69 61).
Open 8am-11pm daily. **Bar**. **Map** p46 B3 ⑦⓪

The most characterful bar on the main square is picked out by the statue of Piotr Skrzynecki, holding a rose and reading Montaigne, sat outside by the cabaret he headed, the Piwnica pod Baranami. Inside is a simple, stand-up place, regulars coming in and out, watched over by caricatures of famous local figures. Few tourists bother with it, a plus point considering the location.

Wentzl

Wentzl Hotel, Rynek Główny 19 (012 429 57 12). **Open** 1pm-midnight daily. **Restaurant**. **Map** p46 C3 ⑦①

Another landmark on the main square, this hotel-restaurant with more than 200 years of history behind it (note the sign outside denoting 1792) understandably sticks with tradition where food is concerned. House specialities include crayfish soup with trout dumplings, and fillet of deer with fresh rosemary in morel sauce – game features prominently. It would be a shame not to follow these with an equally classic dessert, namely the Wentzl strudel of figs, apples or plums.

Wesele

NEW *Rynek Główny 10 (012 422 74 60).* **Open** 11am-11pm daily. **Restaurant**. **Map** p46 C3 ⑦②

The most significant local restaurant opening of 2008, named after the Wyspiański play ('Wedding'), Wesele comes from the same stable as the popular Miód Malina nearby. Set on the St Mary's side of the main square, its perfect location is matched by the quality of its kitchen. In a two-floor rustic interior, diners are treated to Polish classics in stunning sauces – the honey mustard complementing the smoked pork joint, for example, or honey and red wine on the recommended goose breast. Wine runs from an affordable house Mendoza to quality Barolos and Chablis, and there is occasional vocal or acoustic accompaniment.

Wierzynek

Rynek Główny 15 (012 424 96 00).
Open 1pm-midnight daily.
Restaurant. **Map** p46 C3 ⑦③

You don't get more traditional than this – royals and world leaders have eaten here since the merchant of the same name hosted a banquet for Casimir the Great in 1364. Suckling pig, country goose and haunches of veal typify the historic menu of head chef Marcin Sołtys – even the standard one includes dishes such as saddle of deer with juniper seasoning. You could spend wisely or spend a fortune – the historic set menu is 185zł.

Wiśniowy Sad

Grodzka 33 (012 430 21 11). **Open** 11am-10pm Mon-Thur; 11am-midnight Fri-Sun. **Café-restaurant. Map** p47 C4 **74**

The 'Cherry Orchard', hidden inside an old house on Grodzka, is somewhere Chekhov's storytelling mother might have appreciated: samovar, candles, crochet tablecloths and an old piano in the corner for Russian favourites on weekend evenings. The borsch, Siberian *pel'meni* and sweet or savoury *vareniki* pancakes are all fresh and home-made. Open with caviar and vodka and finish with the house cake of cottage cheese and tea flavoured with cherry jam. Despite their limited English, staff are friendly and helpful.

Zapiecek Polskie Pierogarnie

Sławkowska 32 (012 422 74 95). **Open** 8am-10pm daily. **Restaurant. Map** p46 C1 **75**

Pierogi dumplings of every stuffing known to Poland are served through a little hatch to bemused backpackers and local regulars happy for their usual under-ten złoty steaming fill-up. Sweet or savoury, meaty or mushroomy, heavy bowlfuls are ladled out by a muscular lady of a certain age as essential to the place as the rustic furniture.

Zakopianka

Św Marka 34 (012 421 40 45). **Open** 10am-11pm daily. **Café. Map** p46 D2 **76**

The nicest place on Planty for a drink, this 175-year-old café exudes a timeless feel. Comfortable inside and out, it is named after the road between Krakow and Zakopane as travellers would meet here before setting off for the hills.

Księgarnia Hetmańska p69

KRAKOW BY AREA

Punkt p70

Shopping

Alhena

Pl Mariacki 1 (012 421 54 96/www. alhena.pl). **Open** 10am-6pm Mon-Fri; 11am-3pm Sat. **Map** p46 C2 ⑰

All the top names in Polish glass are carried here – Kryształek, Krosno, Tarnów – for decorative and kitchenware, in a prime location.

Cloth Hall

Rynek Główny (no phone). **Open** 10am-8pm daily. **Map** p46 C3 ⑱

Combine sightseeing and souvenir shopping at this ever-busy centrepiece in the main square, lined with stalls proffering toys, embroidery, leather goods, candles and wooden artefacts. Goods tend to be of reasonable quality, but do check the labels first.

Desa

Floriańska 13 (012 421 89 87/www. desa.art.pl). **Open** 11am-7pm Mon-Fri; 11am-2pm Sat. **Map** p46 C2 ⑲

The main office of this long-established antiques firm, with branches dotted about the Old Town, stages regular auctions at this two-floor venue. This outlet specialises in icons, silverware and Polish art, but there's enough here to merit a good, long, general browse.

Empik

Rynek Główny 5 (012 423 81 90/www. empik.com). **Open** 9am-10pm daily. **Map** p46 C3 ⑳

The main outlet in the city for contemporary media is set in a prominent building near St Mary's. A lift swishes shoppers between floors of books, DVDs, CDs, stationery and photo equipment. The ground floor fills with tourists browsing international magazines, the internet café on the third keeps longer hours than most in town and there is also a ticket outlet for concerts and events.

Femini

Św Jana 5 (012 429 19 83/www. femini.pl). **Open** 10am-6pm Mon-Fri; 10am-2pm Sat. **Map** p46 C2 ㉛

One of Krakow's brightest boutiques for contemporary women's clothes displays the neat cuts and classy frills of Krakow pair Monika Pietrzak-Szlęk and Katarzyna Wilk-Filipowicz, regular participants at London Fashion Week. Dresses, tops, skirts and even bridal wear are ranged over their main outlet here.

Galeria Dom Polski

Pl Mariacki (012 431 16 77/www. galeriadp.com). **Open** 9am-6pm Mon-Sat; 9am-3pm Sun. **Map** p46 C2 ⓷²
If you're looking for that individual souvenir, this bright boutique sharing the same roof as Krakow's most central tourist information office is the best port of call. Displaying individual and unusual works by a select handful of local artists – the succint, striking knick-knacks of Karolina Nowysz, the bawdy figures of Ada Bystrzycka – the 'Polish Home Gallery' offers decorative household items with style and taste.

Galeria Osobliwości

Sławkowska 16 (012 429 19 84/www. este.krakow.pl). **Open** 11am-7pm Mon-Fri; 11am-3pm Sat. **Map** p46 C2 ⓷³
For the best part of 20 years, Zbylut and Katarzyna Grzywacz have been collecting and trading exotic and unusual items from around the world – theirs is a real 'Gallery of Curiosities', in fact. Butterflies, shells, art from Oceania, insects trapped in amber, wood carvings from Africa; the term 'eclectic' doesn't really do it justice.

Galeria Plakatu

Stolarska 8-10 (012 421 26 40/www. cracowpostergallery.com). **Open** 10am-5pm Mon-Sat; 11am-2pm Sun. **Map** p46 C3 ⓷⁴
Some 800 posters by 30 Polish artists – for cabaret shows (Wiktor Górka), plays (Ryszard Kaja) and film festivals (Jan Lenica) – are sold at this store near the Maly Rynek. Check out Swava Harasymowicz's illustrations for local showings of *Mulholland Drive*. There are none by humorist Andrzej Mleczko, who has his own gallery of posters and postcards at Św Jana 14 (012 421 71 04).

Galeria RA/Baltic Amber

Floriańska 30 (012 431 16 83). **Open** 10am-7pm Mon-Sat. **Map** p46 C2 ⓷⁵

Maria Radziszewska's store goes under a couple of names but there is no mistaking the craftsmanship and invention of her jewellery. The Old Town has at least a dozen boutiques proffering the local product of amber – this one is a cut above.

Hexeline

Rynek Główny 11 (012 429 43 76/www. hexe.com.pl). **Open** 9.30am-7pm Mon-Fri; 10am-2pm Sat. **Map** p46 C3 ⓷⁶
Perhaps the most successful figure in ladies' fashion is Halina Zawadzka, the driving force behind this enviably successful brand. For two decades or more, women across Poland have opted for Hexeline's look, classy and sharp, suitable for work or pleasure, produced in half-yearly seasons.

Kopernik Toruńskie Pierniki

Grodzka 14 (012 431 13 06/www. kopernik.com.pl). **Open** 9am-7pm Mon-Fri; 9am-3pm Sat. **Map** p46 C3 ⓷⁷
Forget Nuremberg, say the Poles – Toruń is the home of gingerbread. Thus the main producers from this pretty town near Krakow can also trade on the name of their most celebrated son, Copernicus, and decorate their boxes with shooting stars. Look out for gingerbread models of famous local houses, real works of art.

Księgarnia Hetmańska

Rynek Główny 17 (012 430 24 53/www. hetmanska.pl). **Open** 9am-9pm Mon-Sat; 11am-9pm Sun. **Map** p46 C3 ⓷⁸
In the historic townhouse that accommodated the Royal Mint in the 1500s, Hetmańska is a lovely emporium of colourful children's books and puzzles, atlases and souvenir photo albums of old Krakow. If you're looking for a globe, go no further. It is divided into two sections, with much material in English, and a passageway of tacky souvenirs in between.

Kurant

Rynek Główny 36 (012 422 98 59). **Open** 9am-7pm Mon-Fri; 10am-3pm Sat. **Map** p46 C2 ⓷⁹

KRAKOW BY AREA

This age-old music store has had to move with the times, the editions of Polish jazz and folk now presented and purveyed in CD form. You'll still have to point to the one you want behind a glass case, and pay for it at another desk, but it will make your purchase all that more special.

Likus Concept Store

Pasaż 13, Rynek Główny 13 (012 617 02 50/www.hotel.com.pl). **Open** 9am-9pm Mon-Sat; 11am-5pm Sun. **Map** p46 C3 **90**
The flagship retail outlet for the Likus family operation, occupying the basement of Pasaż 13, the Likus Concept Store comprises the wine boutique Vinoteka 13 and adjoining Bar 13; Delikatessy 13 and its exclusive Polish cold cuts, cheeses and preserves; and the quality clothing and accessories of the LFC Boutique.

Music Corner

Św Tomasza 4 (012 421 82 53/www. musiccorner.pl). **Open** 11am-8pm Mon-Sat; 11am-5pm Sun. **Map** p46 B2 **91**
For all new CD releases, Polish, UK and American, this is the best specialist store in town – jazz, classical and DVDs are stocked too.

Pasaż 13

Pasaż 13, Rynek Główny 13 (012 617 02 27). **Open** 9am-9pm Mon-Sat; 11am-5pm Sun. **Map** p46 C3 **92**
An ambitious concept, Pasaż 13 brings three dozen outlets (Benetton, Cerruti, Rossignol) under one roof in a historic courtyard passage leading from the main square to Stolarska. The basement hosts the four parts of the Likus Concept Store, from the team behind this whole operation.

Punkt

Sławkowska 12 (mobile 0511 56 25 26/www.punkt.sklep.pl). **Open** 10am-7pm Mon-Sat; 11am-4pm Sun. **Map** p46 C2 **93**
Monika Drożyńska's original take on recycling vintage clothes and accessories makes this the most refreshing local brand in town. See box p64.

Sephora

Rynek Główny 5 (012 422 43 05/www. sephora.pl). **Open** 8am-8pm Mon-Sat; 10am-6pm Sun. **Map** p46 C3 **94**
A key carrier of the Helena Rubinstein brand is this prominent branch of the international French chain. The queen of cosmetics was born in a modest house in Kazimierz in 1870.

Szambelan

Gołębie 2 (012 430 24 09/www. szambelan.com.pl). **Open** 8am-8pm Mon-Sat; 11am-6pm Sun. **Map** p46 B3 **95**
As well as a complete range of vodkas, alcoholic rarities such as absinthe and mead are stocked at this handy little boutique just south of the main square.

Tatuum

Rynek Główny 37 (012 431 27 52/www. tatuum.pl). **Open** 10am-8pm Mon-Sat; 10am-6pm Sun. **Map** p46 C2 **96**
Modern-day city and leisure wear for both sexes are produced by this Łódż-based firm, with outlets across Poland and the region, and here on Krakow's main square.

Vistula

Rynek Główny 13 (012 617 02 64/ www.vistula.com.pl). **Open** 9.30am-7pm Mon-Sat; 10am-2pm Sun. **Map** p46 C3 **97**
Clean-cut business suits and smart casual wear for men by Polish brands such as Lettfield and Vesari line this prominent store, one of scores of outlets across Poland.

Wedel

Rynek Główny 46 (012 429 40 85/ www.wedelpijalnie.pl). **Open** 9.30am-6pm Mon-Sat; 10am-3pm Sun. **Map** p46 C2 **98**
Karol Ernest Wedel opened his first chocolate store in Warsaw in the mid 1800s, passing it on to his son Emil, who then passed it on to his son Jan. Nearly 150 years later, the family business was sold to Cadbury, but this classic shop and café thrives according to tradition on the main square. Its main competitor, Wawel, sits at No.33.

Folia Concept Club

Nightlife

Black Gallery
Mikołajska 24 (012 423 00 30). **Open**
4pm-2am Mon-Thur, Sun; 4pm-6am Fri,
Sat. **Map** p46 D3 ❾❾
One of the Old Town's many cellar
bars is a late-night dive frequented by
the pierced, the tattooed and sundry
malcontents. It's not punk as such,
although there is a certain industrial
feel to this three-level booze vortex.

Budda Bar Drink & Garden
Rynek Główny 6 (012 421 65 22).
Open 10am-1am Mon-Fri; noon-1am
Sat, Sun. **Map** p46 C3 ❿❿
All very exotic, even when the action
moves from the garden after October.
In the same building as the Szara
restaurant, right on the square, the
Budda feels somehow naughty and for-
bidden, although it keeps hours more
akin to a standard bar. Sequinned
cushions reflect the multicoloured furnishings beneath images from the
Kama Sutra – something to ponder
over some of the best cocktails in town.

Cień
Św Jana 15 (012 422 21 77). **Open**
8pm-6am Mon-Sat; 8pm-3am Sun.
Map p46 C1 ❿❶

Three bars, two dancefloors and any
number of dimly lit alcoves comprise
this busy cellar club, where house DJs
spin to a smart but up-for-it crowd
through the week. There's a VIP room
and a terrace in summer.

Cztery Pokoje
Gołębie 6 (012 421 10 14). **Open**
8am-1am Mon-Thur; 8am-4am Fri;
10am-4am Sat; 10am-1am Sun.
Map p46 B3 ❿❷
Located in the same courtyard as the
almost-as-popular Boom Bar Rush,
Four Rooms is a pleasing mix of retro
decor and death-wish drinking, much
of it taking place after the witching
hour. Music is almost secondary – people come here to chat and flirt over a
cocktail or two.

Folia Concept Club
NEW *Rynek Główny 30 (012 423 26
52/www.foliaclub.pl).* **Open** 3pm-3am
Mon-Thur, Sun; 3pm-4am Fri, Sat.
Map p46 B2 ❿❸
An ambitious and imaginative attempt
to bring something new to Krakow's
well worn but nonetheless successful
after-hours cellar scene, the arty Folia
attracts off-the-wall types with its
equally off-the-wall decor and agenda
of events. It doesn't spark every night,

the Old Town has too many places for that, but catch it at the right moment and you'll be coming back for more.

Frantic

NEW *Szewska 5 (012 423 04 83).*
Open 6pm-late daily. **Map** p46 B2 **104**
This stretch of Szewska near the main square is crammed with bars and nightspots, mainstream and somewhat silly. Frantic has been a welcome arrival, with quality DJing and a healthy party attitude. Look out for the nights here by the Ministry of Sound.

M Club

Św Tomasza 11A (012 431 00 49).
Open 6pm-4am Wed, Thur; 6pm-5am Fri, Sat. **Map** p46 C2 **105**
The smart M waits on its classy clients from their accompanied entrance past the automatic glass doors to their exit, perhaps three well mixed and efficiently served martinis to the good.

Pauza

Floriańska 18 (012 422 82 58). **Open** 5pm-late daily. **Map** p46 C2 **106**
Ignore your feet suggesting you should head downstairs to yet another Krakow cellar; at Pauza, everything happens upstairs. There an expansive, high-ceilinged space will be dotted with bohemian individuals capable of high-brow cultural chit-chat but who right now would prefer to get off their face. Contemporary decorative touches – note the mini-portraits as you walk in – provide suitable backdrop. Great staff too, manning a long, long bar.

Piękny Pies

Sławkowska 6A (012 421 45 52).
Open 11am-2am Mon-Thur, Sun; 11am-4am Fri, Sat. **Map** p46 B2 **107**
Prime candidate for best nightspot in town, 'the Beautiful Dog' is accessed under a sign for an inferior venue occupying the same corridor. Walk to the back courtyard, cross it and a ragtag of party-minded ne'er-do-wells will be in full swing when you breeze through. Three-deep at the bar, regulars chat and flirt in the back room and, at weekends, gravitate to the basement disco. Upstairs, the music might feature the Mary's, rockabilly or grunge; below, dance tunes from Motown on. Ask a local about the mural, referring to the time the Polish president banished an MP for bringing a dog into parliament.

Pauza

Rdza

Bracka 3-5 (mobile 0600 39 55 41).
Open 7pm-4am Wed-Sat. **Map** p46
B3 **108**

Of the cluster of clubs and bars where Bracka meets the main square, 'Rust' attracts a loyal following. An intimate cellar dotted with enticing alcoves, Rdza lays on a regular programme of Polish and international DJs, its reputation already assuring that the best local ones spin here as often as they can. No stag parties or drunken groups of lads, please.

Showtime

Rynek Główny 28 (012 421 47 14).
Open 7pm-2.30am Mon-Thur, Sun; 7pm-4am Fri, Sat. **Map** p46 B3 **109**

Atop a building of sundry drinkeries, this large haven for funseekers and nighthawks exudes a sense of grandeur: the red carpet up the staircase, the stucco and high ceilings once you arrive. Don't worry, everything's a bit scuffed and lived-in. Grab a chair near the stage (jazz, covers, standards) in the main bar or in the rooms behind, order a reasonably priced beer and let the night take its course.

Arts & leisure

ARS Cinema

Św Jana 6 (012 421 41 99/www.ars.pl).
Open varies. **Map** p46 C2 **110**

Catch a film here (quality mainstream, obscure European) for the historic venue itself – the main screening room, Reduta, was once a ballroom. There are four others under the same roof.

Boogie

Szpitalna 9 (012 429 43 06/www. boogiecafe.pl). **Open** 10am-1am Mon-Wed, Sun; 10am-last guest Thur-Sat. **Map** p46 D2 **111**

After a quick spruce-up in 2008, Boogie can host its regular programme of jazz acts in a pleasant space decorated with portraits of famous past exponents.

Bunkier Sztuki

Pl Szczepański 3A (012 423 09 71/ www.bunkier.com.pl). **Open** 11am-6pm Wed, Fri-Sun; 11am-8pm Thur. **Map** p46 B2 **112**

Opened beside the Palace of Art by the Cultural Ministry in 1950, the Art Bunker hosts a regular programme of challenging shows as well as the World Press Photo exhibition every autumn.

KRAKOW BY AREA

Harris Piano Jazz Bar

Rynek Główny 28 (012 421 57 41/www. harris.krakow.pl). **Open** noon-2am daily. **Map** p46 B3 ⓭

Landmark cellar bar and a major spot on the local music circuit, the HPJB comprises a stage, photos of post-war music stars and a sturdy bar counter, all within a large, dark basement. Themed cocktails (such as a Jazz Scream of vodka, Bailey's, Kahlua and Amaretto) are on offer but most are here to catch a decent Polish live act (jazz, folk or blues) over a beer and still have enough funds to carry the night on elsewhere if so required.

Juliusz Słowacki Theatre

Pl Św Ducha 1 (012 424 45 00/www. slowacki.krakow.pl). **Open** see programme. **Map** p46 D2 ⓮

This sumptuous, fin-de-siècle building set in spacious grounds between Szpitalna and the main station has seen some of the most pivotal moments in Polish theatre – it was here that Wyspiański premièred *The Wedding*, Music and poetry also make the agenda, and the Juliusz Słowacki was home to the Krakow Opera for two years before the Opera House opened in the vicinity in 2008. Most performances are Polish-only, but if you are here for a show, the basement Café Trema is one of the city's most convivial spots.

Kino pod Baranami

Rynek Główny 27 (012 423 07 68/www. kinopodbaranami.pl). **Open** see programme. **Map** p46 B3 ⓯

Krakow's most prominent cinema shows mainly (but not exclusively) Polish-language movies, in three spacious, colour-coded screening rooms. Visiting directors have included Jim Jarmusch and Pedro Almodóvar – expect a few surprise guests for the cinema's 40th anniversary in 2009.

Piwnica pod Baranami

Rynek Główny 27 (012 421 25 00/ www.piwnicapodbaranami.krakow.pl). **Open** *Bar* from 6pm. *Cabaret* from 9pm. **Ticket office** *Św Tomasza 26 (012 421 25 00).* **Map** p46 B3 ⓰

When Piotr Skrzynecki opened a student cabaret here, in the basement of the former 'Palace under the Sign of the Rams', the 1956 Hungarian Uprising had just been quashed. For the next 40 years until his death in 1997, the Piwnica pod Baranami continually staged off-the-wall and radical performances, something risky and unique in Communist Poland – little was sacred. Shows still run here, on Saturday nights in winter and more often in summer, when the month-long Krakow Jazz Festival also takes place.

Stalowe Magnolie

Św Jana 15 (012 422 84 72/www. stalowemagnolie.com). **Open** 6pm-2am Mon-Thur, Sun; 6pm-4am Fri, Sat. **Map** p46 C2 ⓱

Jazz singers and small combos entertain guests in this red-lit, bare-brick venue, with waitress-service and pricey cocktails. The management also runs the classy Piano Rouge on the main square (No.46, 012 431 03 33), of similar ilk and price range.

Stary Theatre

Jagiellońska 5 (012 422 85 66/www. stary-teatr.pl). **Open** see programme. **Map** p46 B2 ⓲

Krakow's oldest cultural institution, founded around the time of the French Revolution, has had a patchwork history, outlined in its little museum. Also downstairs is the Café Maska, reason alone to visit – or if your Polish is up to local-language versions of Racine, Shakespeare and Molière.

U Muniaka

Floriańska 3 (012 423 12 05/www. umuniaka.krakow.pl). **Open** 7pm-2am daily. **Map** p46 C2 ⓳

A programme of reliably decent jazz takes place here most nights at 9.30pm, thanks to the influence and dedication of legendary local saxophonist Janusz Muniak, who founded the club in 1992. The setting couldn't be better either, a historic townhouse within earshot of St Mary's bugle. There's a decent kitchen as well as the standard range of drinks and cocktails.

plac Nowy

Kazimierz & Stradom

Pre-Spielberg, visitors to the old Jewish quarter of **Kazimierz** would have found a ghost town of grey, empty streets. If someone had said that the desolate market square of plac Nowy would later become the most exciting bar hub in Poland, if not Central Europe, it would have been dismissed as pure fantasy. It took the success of *Schindler's List* and resurgence of Jewish culture from the mid 1990s on for this fantasy to become fact.

Around plac Nowy, all but one of the half-dozen synagogues, where a faith and community once thrived alongside a Christian one, is a museum. Quality restaurants, particularly on and off the main street/square of Szeroka, abound.

And it's not just Jewish culture. Here in this tiny hub criss-crossed with residential streets you can find cuisine from Argentina to Cuba, and vodka practically round the clock. Between Kazimierz and the Old Town, a kind of no-man's-land partly referred to as **Stradom**, a random building was taken over as party central in 2002: Wielopole 15. Partygoers find themselves flitting between there, Kazimierz and the Old Town, hopping on trams between them or chucking 10zł at a taxi driver to shuttle between Rynek Główny and the rank on the corner of plac Nowy and Estery.

The rest of Stradom comprises stately 19th-century buildings, one housing the new **Aquarium**.

Sights & museums

Aquarium/Natural History Museum

NEW *Św Sebastiana 9 (012 429 10 40/ www.aquariumkrakow.pl). Tram 6, 8, 10, 18.* **Open** 9am-8pm Mon-Fri; 9am-9pm Sat, Sun. **Admission** 22zł; 17zł reductions; 10zł 3-16s. Under-3s free. **Map** p77 A2 ①

Krakow's newest attraction is the brainchild of reptile fan Nathan, owner of nearby Nathan's Villa Hostels. Linking with the Natural History Museum, Nathan is looking to expand the operations of this venerable, tiled institution to include Poland's biggest, shark-filled, aquarium. For the time being, until the summer of 2009, the limited collection includes piranhas, clown fish and sea horses. The snakes, lizards and tropical reptiles remain in their heated quarters upstairs; below is the 23,000-year-old hairy rhino found in southern Poland, a fixture here since 1930. A ticket price of 18zł (12zł reductions) is in place until summer.

City Engineering Museum

Św Wawrzyńca 15 (012 421 12 42/ www.mimk.com.pl). Tram 3, 13, 24. **Open** *Oct-May* 10am-4pm Tue-Sun. *June-Sept* 10am-6pm Tue, Thur; 10am-4pm Wed, Fri-Sun. **Admission** 6.50zł; 4.50zł reductions; 10zł 3-16s. **Map** p77 B4 ②

Set around the sheds and grounds of an old tram depot, this child-friendly interactive attraction allows young visitors to make things wizz, connect and light up. Dads might like the display of Polski Fiats from 1936 to 2000.

Corpus Christi Church

Bożego Ciała 25 (no phone). Tram 6, 8, 10. **Open** 9am-7pm Mon-Sat. **Admission** free. **Map** p77 B4 ③

In place since Casimir's reign in the 1300s, battered and subsequently rebuilt after various invasions, this imposing Gothic edifice is no beauty but features two oddities: a mini Gethsemane, caged and fixed to an outer wall; and a boat-shaped pulpit in the Baroque interior.

Aquarium

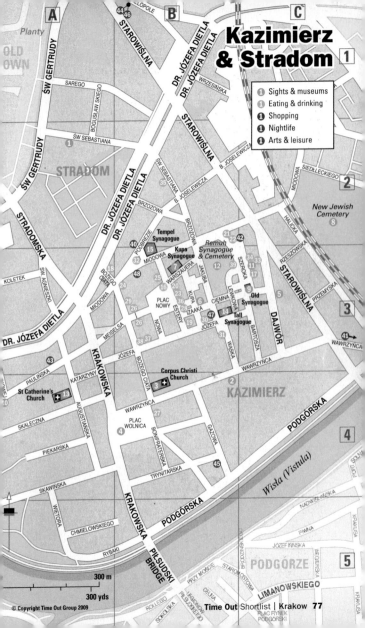

Kazimierz & Stradom

Planty
OLD TOWN
STRADOM
New Jewish Cemetery
Tempel Synagogue
Kupa Synagogue
Remuh Synagogue & Cemetery
Old Synagogue
Tall Synagogue
Corpus Christi Church
KAZIMIERZ
St Catherine's Church
PLAC NOWY
PLAC WOLNICA
Wisła (Vistula)
PILSUDSKI BRIDGE
PODGÓRZE

Legend

1 Sights & museums
1 Eating & drinking
1 Shopping
1 Nightlife
1 Arts & leisure

300 m
300 yds

Airline flights are one of the biggest producers of the global warming gas CO_2. But with **The CarbonNeutral Company** you can make your travel a little greener.

Go to **www.carbonneutral.com** to calculate your flight emissions then 'neutralise' them through international projects which save exactly the same amount of carbon dioxide.

Contact us at **shop@carbonneutral.com** or call into the office on **0870 199 99 88** for more details.

CarbonNeutral®flights

Ethnographic Museum

Pl Wolnica 1 (012 430 60 23/www. etnomuzeum.eu). Tram 6, 8, 10. **Open** 11am-7pm Tue, Wed, Fri, Sat; 11am-9pm Thur; 11am-3pm Sun. **Admission** 8zł; 4zł reductions. **Map** p77 B4 **④**

Don't be put off by the old-school staff and stuffy ambience – this three-floor museum is well worth investigating. Downstairs are models and mock-ups of five typical peasant cottages in southern Poland. Rural life is outlined in equally exhaustive detail upstairs, from cradle to grave, via childhood, school, farm labour, military service, church, marriage, music, cooking, celebrations and pastimes. Much is labelled in English. Art and pottery are showcased on the top floor of this former town hall building.

Galicia Jewish Museum

Dajwór 18 (012 421 68 42/www. galiciajewishmuseum.org). Tram 3, 13, 24. **Open** 10am-6pm daily. **Admission** 12zł; 6zł reductions. **Map** p77 C3 **⑤**

British photographer Chris Schwarz and historian Jonathan Webber toured southern Poland (Galicia) to record its ruined synagogues and hidden sites of anti-Semitic murder. The result is a stark reminder, in black and white, with bilingual documentation, that the Holocaust involved the casual slaying of Jews by disgruntled villagers and passing Nazis. Also gripping is the brave story of the underground Jewish Resistance in Krakow. Unmissable.

Isaak Synagogue

Kupa 18 (012 430 22 22). Tram 6, 8, 10. **Open** 10am-4pm Mon-Thur, Sun; 10am-noon Fri. **Admission** 5zł; 2zł reductions. **Map** p77 B3 **⑥**

Behind its impressive loggia façade, this is another local synagogue transformed into a museum. The beautiful 17th- and 18th-century murals are a recent discovery; the chilling newsreel films of Nazi round-ups in these streets 70 years ago are sadly also authentic.

Kupa Synagogue

Miodowa 27 (no phone). Tram 6, 8, 10. **Open** 9am-6pm Mon-Fri, Sun. **Admission** free. **Map** p77 B3 **⑦**

More recently uncovered murals of biblical tales make the Kupa a pleasant stopover on any walking tour of the Jewish quarter.

Galicia Jewish Museum

KRAKOW BY AREA

New Jewish Cemetery

Miodowa 55 (no phone). Tram 3, 9, 11, 13, 24. **Open** 9am-4pm Mon-Fri, Sun. **Admission** free. **Map** p77 C2 ⑧

Vast and overgrown, this site is still in use but mainly contains figures from the 19th century; the main Remuh Cemetery was closed by the Austrians in 1800. The statue to the right as you walk in the main gate is composed of fragmented gravestones and dedicated to victims of Nazi terror.

Old Synagogue

Szeroka 24 (012 422 09 62/www.mhk. pl). Tram 3, 9, 11, 13, 24. **Open** *Nov-Mar* 10am-2pm Mon; 9am-4pm Wed, Thur, Sat, Sun; 10am-5pm Fri. *Apr-Oct* 10am-2pm Mon; 9am-5pm Tue-Sun. **Admission** 8zł; 6zł reductions. Free Mon. **Map** p77 C3 ⑨

Now a branch of the Krakow History Museum, this 16th-century synagogue lay in ruins after the war. Occupying

New Jewish Cemetery

one end of Szeroka, Krakow's oldest synagogue, one part Gothic, one part Renaissance, was restored to house a fascinating collection of local Judaica, focusing mainly on festivals and education. The centrepiece bimah platform is a reconstruction. Note, though, the prayer books, marriage contracts and letters of divorce.

Pauline (Skałka) Church

Skałeczna (012 421 72 44). Tram 18, 19, 22. **Open** 7am-7pm daily. **Admission** free. **Map** p77 A4 ⑩

Off the beaten track and often overlooked, this impressive Baroque church near the river stages outdoor events in summer. Visitors interested in the Młoda Polska movement of the late 1800s might care to see the tomb of Stanisław Wyspiański in the crypt.

Popper Synagogue

Szeroka 24 (012 421 29 87). Tram 3, 9, 11, 13, 24. **Open** 9am-6pm Mon-Fri, Sun. **Admission** free. **Map** p77 C3 ⑪

Tucked away behind the restaurants of Szeroka, this brightly coloured arts centre for local youngsters was once the grandest synagogue in Krakow, built in 1620 by a legendary banker named Popper.

Remuh Synagogue & Cemetery

Szeroka 40 (012 429 57 35). Tram 3, 9, 11, 13, 24. **Open** 9am-4pm Mon-Fri, Sun. **Admission** 5zł; 2zł reductions. concs **Map** p77 B3 ⑫

An essential stop on any Jewish tour of Kazimierz, the Remuh comprises a cramped synagogue, still in use, and the resting place of Krakow's leading Jews from 1552 to 1800. Many tombs were smashed by the Nazis during the war, the fragments painstakingly fitted together to form a wailing wall you see to the right as you enter.

St Catherine's Church

Augustiańska 7 (012 430 62 42). Tram 6, 8, 10, 18, 19, 22. **Open** 10am-3pm Mon-Fri; 10am-2pm Sat; 1.30-5pm Sun. **Admission** free. **Map** p77 A4 ⑬

Reborn and revived

Jewish Cultural Festival

It was 20 years ago that a Catholic with an interest in Judaism, Pole Janusz Makuch, started a modest event, almost underground, of klezmer music and Jewish culture. A few hundred showed up, happy to find that authentic musicians not only survived the war and its aftermath, but were still playing.

A year later, the Wall fell but here there was no great goldrush or overnight property boom. Much of Krakow – and certainly the old Jewish sites of Kazimierz and Podgórze – remained untouched.

This was the raw material that author Thomas Keneally and Steven Spielberg found to tell their stories of the Holocaust, its heroes and survivors, in Krakow.

When Spielberg came here to shoot in 1993, he was delighted to discover that klezmer music had also survived. At the film's Polish première at Kino Kijów, the director leapt onstage to give an impromptu blast on the saxophone alongside singer Irena Urbanska and her klezmer band.

And although Kazimierz was still grim and dilapidated, shoots were beginning to grow. The **Jewish Culture Festival** was taking shape, attracting thousands and stretching events (music, film, exhibitions) over a set nine-day period. Tourists began to traipse around the Schindler sights. With money coming in, the synagogues were slowly renovated and turned into museums – with freedom of enterprise, bars started opening amid the boarded-up buildings and bric-a-brac shops.

After **Alchemia** (p82) and **Singer** (p87), a bar scene grew around plac Nowy. Festivalgoers flocked in larger numbers. By 2007, 40,000 came, 13,000 for the finale, 'Shalom on Szeroka'. Makuch got the Poland Reborn award from Polish president Lech Kaczyński.

The musicians worked year-round at Alchemia and Drukarnia: Holocaust survivors like Leopold Kozlowski; and experimental outfits like Krokke, whose occasional member was new Krakow resident Nigel Kennedy.

Today Kazimierz is the liveliest place to be, the venues so thick on the ground that the Drukarnia moved over the river to Podgórze, site of the wartime Jewish Ghetto.

KRAKOW BY AREA

Tempel Synagogue

Part Gothic, part Baroque, and dating back to the 1300s, St Catherine's is notable for the late Gothic murals in the cloisters – much was lost during its stint as a warehouse in the 1800s.

Tall Synagogue

Józefa 38 (012 426 75 20). Tram 6, 8, 10. **Open** *Winter* 9am-5pm Mon-Fri, Sun. *Summer* 9am-7pm Mon-Fri, Sun. **Admission** 9zł; 6zł reductions. **Map** p77 B3 ⑭

Behind a shabby façade where Józefa meets Jakuba, this first-floor prayer room shows a 17th-century portal but sadly little else after its wartime ruin.

Tempel Synagogue

Miodowa 24 (012 429 57 35). Tram 6, 8, 10, 19, 22. **Open** 9am-4pm Mon-Fri, Sun. **Admission** 5zł; 2zł reductions. **Map** p77 B3 ⑮

The stained-glass windows provide the backdrop for the annual Jewish Culture Festival; and tell of Tempel's role as an inclusive, forward-looking synagogue from the 1860s to 1939.

Eating & drinking

Alchemia

Estery 5 (012 421 22 00/www. alchemia.com.pl). Tram 6, 8, 10. **Open** 10am-4am Mon; 9am-4am Tue-Sun. **Bar-club. Map** p77 B3 ⑯

Landmark bar on the busiest corner of plac Nowy, Alchemia was essential to the late blossoming of Kazimierz. Elements included a scuffed wooden interior, counter service and improbably late hours. You can expect the same today only now everyone and their uncle knows about it.

Ariel

Szeroka 17-18 (012 421 79 20/www. ariel-krakow.pl). Tram 3, 9, 11, 13, 24. **Open** 10am-11pm daily. **Restaurant. Map** p77 C3 ⑰

Homely yet always full of tourists, Ariel means hearty helpings of Jewish favourites – Sephardic carp, *cholent*, dumplings – served by staff far too clever for their own good.

Avocado

*Bożego Ciała 1 (012 422 04 86/www.
restoavocado.pl). Tram 19, 22.* **Open**
8am-11pm daily. **Restaurant. Map**
p77 A3 ⑱

Despite its cosmopolitan appearance,
Avocado offers mainly domestic dishes with few surprises (herring in sour
cream, duck in wine-and-honey sauce)
– but it's a pleasant and reasonably
priced spot nonetheless.

Buena Vista

*Józefa 26 (mobile0668 035 000/www.
buenavista.krakow.pl). Tram 6, 8, 10.*
Open noon-1am Mon-Thur, Sun; noon-
2am Fri, Sat. **Bar-restaurant. Map**
p77 B3 ⑲

There's not much Cuban about the
menu filled with tapas standards (tor-
tilla, paella, calamares) but the cocktails (mojitos, daiquiris, ice teas) mixed
with Havana Club, Finlandia and other
quality brands make for a pleasant pit-
stop right on plac Nowy.

Les Couleurs

*Estery 10 (012 429 42 70). Tram 6, 8,
10.* **Open** 7am-midnight Mon-Thur;
7am-2am Fri; 8am-2am Sat; 8am-
midnight Sun. **Café**. No credit cards.
Map p77 B3 ⑳

The day starts here with Wi-Fi, fresh
juice and croissants, and finishes with
booze hounds of both sexes pounding
back the *piwo* at the zinc bar counter.
Day-long chatter echoes around this
recognisably French café interior, featuring a Gainsbourg-sized bottle of
Pernod and images of the man himself.

Dawno temu
na Kazimierzu

*Szeroka 1 (012 421 21 17). Tram 3, 9,
11, 13, 24.* **Open** 10am-11pm daily.
Restaurant. Map p77 B2 ㉑

This reconstruction of pre-war shops
and workshops, displaying the ethnic
mix of the day, is more tourist sight
than locale but the garlic-and-tarragon
soup or fried liver with boletus mushrooms make for a welcoming meal all
the same. The name, over shopkeepers'
signs both Jewish and Christian, means
'Once Upon a Time in Kazimierz'.

Klezmer Hois

*Szeroka 6 (012 411 12 45/www.
klezmer.pl). Tram 3, 9, 11, 13, 24.*
Open 10am-10pm daily. **Restaurant.
Map** p77 B2 ㉒

If anything points to the Jewish revival
in these parts, it's this haven of age-old

Manzana p84

KRAKOW BY AREA

Nova p85

cuisine, vivacious banter and nightly live klezmer music. Tourists flock to the place but the music, like the food, is authentic – and guarantees a grand time had by all.

Królicze Oczy

Estery 14 (012 431 10 31). Tram 6, 8, 10. **Open** 10am-2am Mon-Thur, Sun; 10am-4am Fri, Sat. **Bar**. No credit cards. **Map** p77 B3 ㉓
Rabbit's Eyes is a boho plac Nowy bar done out with early erotica, found furniture and other decoration more suited to a squat party. A nice alternative to the trendier spots alongside.

Manzana

Miodowa 11 (012 422 77 77/www.manzana.com.pl). Tram 3, 9, 11, 13, 24. **Open** 7am-11pm daily. **Bar-restaurant**. **Map** p77 B3 ㉔
Latin-themed, Manzana is better than the lame etchings on its front windows ('Tacos Durango', 'Pescado Blanco') would have you believe. Divided between cocktail bar and restaurant, with a menu partly shared between the two, this sleek operation can provide you with chicken diabolo of spicy risotto as well as a Mexican martini with top-class tequila or Mescal.

Miejsce

Estery 1 (mobile 0783 096 016/www.miejsce.com.pl). Tram 6, 8, 10. **Open** 10am-2am Mon-Wed, Sun; 10am-3am Thur-Sat. **Bar**. No credit cards. **Map** p77 B3 ㉕
This unpretentious retro bar just off plac Nowy attracts a fair mix of arty types and students, and, pleasingly, few stag-weekending idiots – there's little evidence of a bar sign outside.

Mleczarnia

Meiselsa 20 (012 421 85 32/www.mlie.pl). Tram 3, 9, 11, 13, 24. **Open** 8am-2am Mon-Thur, Sun; 8am-4am Fri, Sat. **Café**. **Map** p77 B3 ㉖
There are two Mleczarnias: summer and winter. In summer, a terrace one spreads over a sizeable space by Józefa to create the best alfresco drinking space in Kazimierz; year-round, a tatty junk shop of a bar opposite offers the same drinks in bohemian surrounds.

Młynek

Pl Wolnica 7 (012 430 62 02). Tram 6, 8, 10. **Open** 10am-late daily. **Café**. **Map** p77 B4 ㉗
Garbo and Marilyn gaze from the counter of this cosy, two-space café, separated by a passageway, over

which a spritely waitress brings house breakfasts of scrambled eggs, house cocktails of vodka, Campari and juices, hot apple pies, steaming bowls of *bigos* stew, and, most frequently, coffees, beers or wine. Cultural magazines and occasional readings or slide shows lend the place an arty edge.

Nova

Estery 18 (012 421 40 11/www.nova restobar.pl). Tram 6, 8, 10. Open 9am-midnight daily. **Bar-restaurant**. **Map** p77 B3 ㉘

Lounge bar and restaurant, the modern, spacious Nova on the corner of plac Nowy provides satisfying sustenance, from breakfast (eg an 'English' of sausage, omelette and shallow-cooked mushrooms); to lunch (seafood pappardelle); to dinner (rib-eye steak with tabasco), with snacks (ciabatta melts) in between. Nowhere near as upscale as it thinks it is, but none the worse for all that. Nice for drinks too.

Pieroźka u Vincenta

Bożego Ciała 12 (mobile 0501 747 407). Tram 6, 8, 10, 19, 22. Open noon-8pm Mon-Thur, Sun; noon-10pm Fri, Sat. **Restaurant**. **Map** p77 B3 ㉙

Apart from a reprint of his starry sky on the wall of the adjoining extra dining area, Vincent the artist has little in common with the humble Polish dumpling dish, the only dining option here. This modest *pierogi* establishment (pierogeria?) carries on regardless, serving 30 varieties, both sweet (orange and agaric mushroom) and strange (chicken liver and apple).

Pimento

Józefa 26 (012 421 25 02/www. pimento.pl). Tram 3, 9, 11, 13, 24. **Open** noon-11pm daily. **Restaurant**. **Map** p77 B3 ㉚

This swish, two-floor Argentine grill serves steaks in a dozen sizes, cooked to your wishes and choice of sauce – chimichurri suits a medium Morocha. It's not cheap but you're paying for imported beef and you can see your quarry being prepared from the comfort of your picture-window seat.

Portofino

Wąska 2 (012 431 05 37/www. portofino.pl). Tram 3, 9, 11, 13, 24. **Open** 10am-11pm Mon-Thur, Sun; 10am-midnight Fri, Sat. **Restaurant**. **Map** p77 B3 ㉛

High Fidelity p89

KRAKOW BY AREA

The top terrace in Kazimierz catches the afternoon sun as you tuck into Polish favourites (*żurek* soup, tenderloin in Żubrówka vodka sauce) or pasta standards (gnocchi in mushroom sauce, cannelloni with spinach and salmon). Prices are reasonable and lunchtime can linger to late afternoon.

Propaganda

Miodowa 20 (012 292 04 02). Tram 6, 8, 10. **Open** 11am-3am Mon-Thur, Sun; 11am-5am Fri, Sat. **Bar**. No credit cards. **Map** p77 B3 ③

Spend a long night's journey into day at this dark cabin of a place, done out with paraphernalia from the Commie days. This is no lame theme bar either – locals lash back beers and chasers while a party-minded barman cranks up the punk, metal or grunge.

Ptasiek

Dajwór 3 (012 431 03 41/www.ptasiek. eu). Tram 3, 9, 11, 13, 24. **Open** 3pm-midnight Mon-Thur, Sun; 3pm-2am Thur, Fri. **Bar**. **Map** p77 C3 ③

A quiet place for a board game or web surf over a coffee or glass of Guinness, the 'Little Bird' is a relaxed spot whose garden comes to the fore in summer.

Rubinstein

Rubinstein Hotel, Szeroka 12 (012 384 00 07). Tram 3, 9, 11, 13, 24. **Open** noon-10pm daily. **Restaurant**. **Map** p77 C3 ③

The best hotel-restaurant in Kazimierz, named after the beautician who lived here, offers three kinds of menu sprinkled with the invention of chef Mariusz Glac. A 140zł tasting selection involves sea fish and prosciutto in pepper-and-tomato sauce; ostrich is the stand-out on the standard menu; while the quarterly one provides the venue with its new name of the Four Seasons.

San Sebastián Café

Św Sebastiana 25 (012 429 24 76/ www.sansebastian.pl). Tram 19, 22. **Open** 8am-11pm Mon-Sat; 9am-11pm Sun. **Pub-restaurant**. **Map** p77 B2 ③

More pub than café, this busy Stradom eaterie provides a handy stopover if you're walking to Kazimierz from the Old Town, maybe for a hearty meal (pork knuckle cooked in beer), a grilled chicken ciabatta or a glass of wine from Sicily or Israel. Not a spot for the whole night – it's too far from the action, unless that's just what you're after.

Galeria Kazimierz p89

Jarden Jewish Bookshop p89

Singer

Estery 20 (012 292 06 22). Tram 6, 8, 10. **Open** 9am-3am Mon-Thur, Sun; 9am-5am Fri, Sat. **Bar**. No credit cards. **Map** p77 B3 ③⑥

Sewing machines were never put to such good use than as bar tables here. Along with Alchemia, this spot kick-started plac Nowy to be the bustling bar hub of today. No one bustles here, though – they sip flavoured vodkas and chat in a boudoir atmosphere. Seats outside catch the afternoon sun.

Stajnia

Józefa 12 (012 423 72 02/www.pub stajnia.pl). Tram 6; 8, 10. **Open** 11am-1am Mon-Wed, Sun; 11am-2am Thur; 11am-4am Fri, Sat. **Bar-restaurant**. No credit cards. **Map** p77 B3 ③⑦

Set in the courtyard where Spielberg shot a famous scene from *Schindler's List*, this otherwise unremarkable hostelry gets more than its fair share of tourists. Inside, the pub continues its 'Stable' theme; outside, wicker chairs spread over the cobbled, characterful space, convivial for a beer or pizza.

Starka

NEW *Józefa 14 (012 430 65 38/ www.starka.com.pl). Tram 6, 8, 10.* **Open** noon-11pm daily. **Bar-restaurant**. **Map** p77 B3 ③⑧

Full marks to Starka! Quality goulash, turkey steak and Cracow cheesecake with raspberry sauce match your choice from a full range of vodkas, including the dry, titular variety made of rye grain, in vintages up to 25 years. Prints of Heinrich Zille's caricatures line the bright red walls, the atmosphere intimate in the darker back room.

Szara Kazimierz

NEW *Szeroka 39 (012 429 12 19). Tram 3, 9, 11, 13.* **Open** 11am-11pm daily. **Restaurant**. **Map** p77 B3 ③⑨

Recently opened cousin of the famous restaurant in the Old Town, SK offers a less formal, but by no means poorer, dining experience than on the main market square. Daily specials are chalked up, meats with tasty sides and sauces, at prices you would pay in a far less desirable location than this prime spot right on Szeroka.

KRAKOW BY AREA

House party

Łubu-Dubu

Krakow has no air-hangar disco or superclub. Perhaps locals don't need one – certainly the Old Town or Kazimierz don't have the available space anyway. What Krakow does have is an all-in-one party zone occupying a single house: **Wielopole 15**.

Leaving the Old Town from the market square past Szara down Sienna, you reach the tram-lined ring road and, at the Post Office, a fork. Take the left-hand and, past the Holiday Inn on the other side, you'll see party-minded types staggering in or out of an open doorway. There is rarely any goon on the door. Entry fees are only charged for special events. This is all-night bar-hopping at its cheapest and most convenient. Walk in, and you are drawn to the indie blast coming out of **Playground**. Scale one floor higher and there's the retro heaven of **Łubu-Dubu** (p90) and, opposite, the edgier **Caryca** (no, it's not a bordello). Climb higher to the top and... ta-daa! **Kitsch** (p89), camp and tacky, is a convivial gay/straight mix of party-minded mingling and the occasional show.

Punters switch from spot to spot, like rooms at a house party – if there's a foxy crowd at one or better sounds at another, they stick around. Things wind down around tram time or dawn.

It all started in 2002, when an original student club, Łubu-Dubu, was opened in an empty building. Ten years after Communism was a healthy enough period for students to appreciate the value in a retro drinking bar – and Jarosław Daniel and team had found boyhood souvenirs from Poland's 1974 World Cup campaign, signs, badges, and so on. The tolerant atmosphere, on a dim street where many would have feared to tread, encouraged Zenek and team to site Kitsch upstairs. Then came the more alternative Caryca.

In 2008, Zenek introduced a gallery inside Caryca, **Moho**, to keep an alternative, creative buzz about the building and offer a popular outlet to young artists. Exhibits survive intact – despite the lakes of (often strong) alcohol consumed, trouble at Wielopole 15 is rare, another attraction for first-time partygoers.

Shopping

High Fidelity

Podbrezie 6 (mobile 0506 184 479).
Tram 19, 22. **Open** noon-5pm Mon-
Sat. **Map** p77 B2/3 ⓸
Hours are flexible here. Music fan Piotr
tries to open at noon and keep running
until late afternoon. As it's near the
plac Nowy bar scene, in a car-free passage past the Tempel Synagogue, it's
worth popping in to browse the boxes
of jazz and rock vinyl lovingly laid out
in a living-room atmosphere.

Galeria Kazimierz

Podgórska 34 (012 433 01 01/www.
galeriakazimierz.pl). Tram 3, 9, 11, 13,
24. **Open** 10am-10pm Mon-Sat; 10am-
8pm Sun. **Map** p77 C3 ⓶
Down by the river, this 130-store mall
contains the Cinema City multiplex.
Outlets include Timberland, Lego,
Puma and Body Shop plus the usual
plethora of food and drink chains.

Jarden Jewish Bookshop

Szeroka 2 (012 421 71 66/www.
jarden.pl). Tram 3, 9, 11, 13, 24.
Open 9am-6pm Mon-Fri; 10am-6pm
Sat, Sun. **Map** p77 B/C 2/3 ⓷
Both a tour agency (Kazimierz, Jewish
Ghetto, Auschwitz) and bookstore,
Jarden carries some 500 titles on Jewish
themes, 100 of them in English. There
are also maps, CDs and postcards and
clued-in staff can help with queries
about Jewish Krakow.

Nightlife

face2face

Paulińska 28 (www.face2face.krakow.
pl). Tram 18, 19, 22. **Open** from 8pm
daily. No credit cards. **Map** p77 A3 ⓸
Opened in 2008, this candlelit DJ spot
and live (indie, experimental) music cellar has been putting on an eclectic
agenda to lure punters away from the
main Estery/Wielopole beat.

Kitsch

Wielopole 15 (www.kitsch.pl). Tram 1,
3, 7, 13, 19, 24. **Open** from 7pm daily.
No credit cards. **Map** p77 B1 ⓸

face2face

Crowning the all-party building of Wielopole 15, gay-friendly Kitsch is part club, part cabaret, always busy and always fun. See box p88.

Klub Cocon
Gazowa 21 (012 632 22 96/mobile 0501 350 665/www.klub-cocon.pl). Tram 6, 8, 10. **Open** from 9pm Fri, Sat. **Map** p77 B4 ⑤

This lively dance club and cabaret venue saves all its energy for the weekend, when a popular programme of DJs (electro, house) and drag shows entertains a crowd of up-for-it regulars at this riverside spot. Two dark rooms.

Łubu-Dubu
Wielopole 15 (mobile 0694 461 402/ www.lubu-dubu.prv.pl). Tram 1, 3, 7, 13, 19, 24. **Open** 6pm-2am Mon, Tue, Sun; 6pm-3am Wed; 6pm-4am Thur; 6pm-5am Fri, Sat. No credit cards. **Map** p77 B1 ㊻

The most interesting of the Wielopole 15 venues shows lovely retro detail. Friendly staff serve from the crowded main bar – there's a chat and/or dance area either side. See box p88.

Arts & leisure

Kawiarnia Naukowa
Jakuba 29-31 (mobile 0663 833 457/ www.kawiarnianaukowa.ovh.org). Tram 3, 9, 11, 13, 24. **Open** from 6pm daily. No credit cards. **Map** p77 B3 ㊼

Spiky live acts rant and rage in the small side room, drinks flow around the stone bar propped up by a mannequin on a stool and manned by music enthusiasts, and there doesn't seem to be anyone bothering about a cover charge. The pastiche wedding portrait sets the tone.

Krakow Chamber Opera
Miodowa 15 (012 430 66 05/ www.kok.art.pl). Tram 6, 8, 10. **Open** according to programmme. **Map** p77 B3 ㊽

Director Wacław Jankowski and actress Jadwiga Leśniak-Jankowska are the couple behind this 18-year-old venue, also known as the EL JOT Stage Theatre, an attactive and intimate place to catch early Polish music, a recital or sometimes the odd spoken-word performance.

Krakow Chamber Opera

Wawel

Wawel & Waterfront

Poland's holiest and most historic site, Krakow's busiest tourist attraction, looms from atop the south-west corner of the Old Town: **Wawel**. Comprising a **Cathedral**, **Castle** and half a dozen museums, Wawel was where most of Poland's royals were crowned and its rulers sat for 500 years. Then, as now, Church and State are kept separate: visitors to the Cathedral (and its **Museum**) buy tickets from its office opposite its main doors. The adjoining Castle has its office at the main gate halfway up the steep path across Podzamcze from the Old Town; timed tickets for the worthwhile **State Rooms & Royal Apartments**, and **Crown Treasury & Armoury**, are sold there. Get there as soon as you can (numbers are limited, as you'll see from an illuminated ticker) or join one of the many guided tours offered around town.

Below, the Vistula waterfront is sadly underused – although plans are afoot to install a beach area for recreation around the rusting Hotel Forum, by the summer of 2009.

Sights & museums

Cathedral Museum
Wawel 3 (012 429 33 27/www.wawel-krakow.pl). Tram 3, 6, 8, 10, 18, 40. **Open** *Oct-Apr* 9am-4pm Mon-Sat. *May-Sept* 9am-5pm Mon-Sat. **Admission** included with Wawel Cathedral. **Map** p93 B1 ❶

Manggha p95

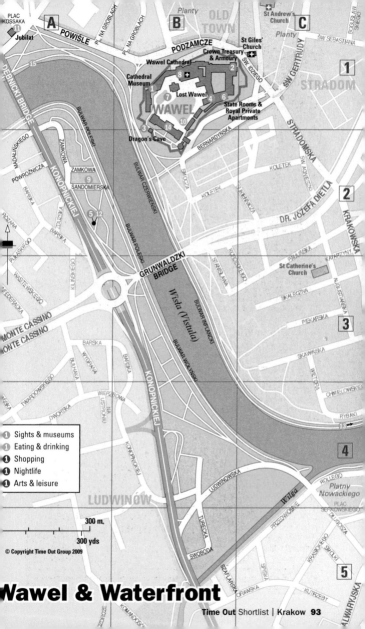

Wawel & Waterfront

Sandy shore

Paris Plage, the Berlin Strand and now... Vistula Sands? Krakow's sadly underused embankment below Wawel Castle and along either shore to Podgórze is being earmarked as an area for riverside recreation in summer.

At the centre of the debate stands the great white elephant of the Socialist era, the **Hotel Forum** (pictured). Looking not unlike the Thunderbirds' headquarters on Tracy Island, this oblong monolith on stilts took a decade to build, from 1978 to 1989 – and another one to close down, owing to poor construction and flooding.

Since 2002, around its base have been set up a go-karting course, paintball sessions and sundry niche pastimes – but developers are now keen to open up Krakow to more mainstream tourism alongside.

Locals too would be happy to see something done with the neglected stretch between Dębniki Bridge to the Grunwaldzki roundabout, at present practically inaccessible to pedestrians. Opposite, on the grass verge under Wawel, punks slug on cans of beer and young lovers entwine. Tourists use the only open-air venue, the **Victoria Pub** boat, while a floating pizzeria further down receives little custom. Similarly, the local water taxis keep a low profile.

On the cards, expected early as 2009, are a beach with a pool, a music bar, an open-air cinema and regular water tram all the way to Tyniec Abbey. Alas, nothing is yet certain on the fate of the Hotel Forum as a whole – a monolith too dear to rebuild and too expensive to demolish.

Set in a little stand-alone house to the right as you enter the Wawel complex, and accessed with your ticket for the Cathedral, this two-floor collection shows coronation robes and insignia of sundry Polish royalty and, above, robes and ornaments relating to Pope John Paul II. Karol Wojtyła himself opened the museum, just before taking the job at the Vatican.

Crown Treasury & Armoury

Wawel 3 (012 422 51 55/www.wawel-krakow.pl). Tram 3, 6, 8, 10, 18, 40. **Open** *Nov-Mar* 9.30am-4pm Tue-Sat. *Apr-Oct* 9.30am-5pm Tue-Fri; 11am-6pm Sat, Sun. **Admission** *Nov-Mar* 14zł; 7zł reductions. *Apr-Oct* 17zł; 10zł reductions. No credit cards. **Map** p93 B1 ❷

Goblets, orbs and jewellery belonging to generations of Polish royals fill one half of this mildly diverting museum, the second of two accessed from the Wawel courtyard. The other half is a chilling collection of medieval instruments of war, evil-looking implements to spear, spike or slay your opponent by the most painful means necessary.

Dragon's Cave

Wawel 3 (012 422 51 55/www.wawel-krakow.pl). Tram 3, 6, 8, 10, 18, 40. **Closed** Nov-Mar. **Open** *Apr-June, Sept, Oct* 10am-5pm daily. *July, Aug* 10am-6pm daily. **Admission** 3zł. Free under-7s. No credit cards. **Map** p93 B1/2 ❸

Smok the dragon is the star here, the spiny creature you'll see hanging from every souvenir stall in town. At this summer-only attraction, kids lead their parents through what seems like miles of ghost train-like passageways (in fact, 160m) before emerging at street level to be scared out of their wits by an actual life-size, fire-breathing Smok. Naturally, they will want to go again – admission is free or nominal.

Lost Wawel

Wawel 3 (012 422 51 55/www.wawel-krakow.pl). Tram 3, 6, 8, 10, 18, 40. **Open** *Nov-Mar* 9.30am-4pm Tue-Sat; 10am-4pm Sun. *Apr-Oct* 9.30am-1pm Mon; 9.30am-5pm Tue-Fri; 11am-6pm Sat, Sun. **Admission** *Nov-Mar* 6zł; 3zł reductions. Free Sun. *Apr-Oct* 8zł; 5zł reductions. Free Mon. No credit cards. **Map** p93 B1 ❹

This often overlooked attraction in a hidden corner of the outer courtyard contains a mixed bag of artefacts from each stage of Wawel's development. The most interesting belong to its pre-Casimir period, the Romanesque remains and models of St Gereon's, the church which also stood here, and whose chapel is still said to emanate waves of positive energy.

Manggha

Konopnickiej 26 (012 267 27 03/www.manggha.krakow.pl). Tram 18, 19, 22. **Open** 10am-6pm Tue-Sun. **Admission** 15zł; 10zł reductions. Free Tue. **Map** p93 A2 ❺

Film director Andrzej Wajda is behind this worthwhile waterfront project, set up with funds he received for a Japanese award in the 1980s. Wajda commissioned Arata Isozaki to create a futuristic home for the 7,000-strong treasure of Japanese woodcut prints, watercolours, antiques and face masks collected by local Feliks Jasieński in the early 20th century. There are also regular contemporary exhibitions by Japanese artists, and a terrace café and sushi bar overlooking the Vistula.

State Rooms & Royal Private Apartments

Wawel 3 (012 422 51 55/www.wawel-krakow.pl). Tram 3, 6, 8, 10, 18, 40. **Open** *Nov-Mar* 9.30am-4pm Tue-Sun. *Apr-Oct* 9.30am-1pm Mon; 9.30am-5pm Tue-Fri; 11am-6pm Sat, Sun. **Admission** *Nov-Mar* 14zł; 7zł reductions. Free Sun. *Apr-Oct* 17zł; 10zł reductions. Free Mon. No credit cards. **Map** p93 B1 ❻

After the Cathedral (and the view), this is reason enough for coming to Wawel. The State Rooms are a series of high-ceilinged, interconnecting rooms decorated with rare Arras tapestries – returned after their wartime evacuation. The Baroque Bird Room with its marble fireplace (1601) is the most impressive space. Visitors to the Royal Private Apartments are given a tour around the sumptuous furnishings belonging to the Polish monarchs. The delicate study in the so-called Hen's Foot Wing is where royal youngsters were given their music lessons.

Wawel Castle

Wawel 3 (012 422 51 55/www.wawel-krakow.pl). Tram 3, 6, 8, 10, 18, 40. **Open** *6am-5pm daily. Office Nov-Mar 9am-4pm daily. Apr-June, Sept, Oct 9am-5pm Mon-Fri; 9am-6pm Sat, Sun. July, Aug 8.15am-6pm daily.* **Map** p93 B1 ❼

Towering between the river and the Old Town, hilltop Wawel Castle is typified by the Gothic appearance granted it by Poland's medieval kings, and its Renaissance makeover in the early 1500s. The Italianate style of its inner courtyard dates from this period, arcaded buildings on three sides housing the State Rooms & Royal Private Apartments, and Crown Treasury & Armoury. Nearer the Cathedral is the outer courtyard, whose look owes more to when the Habsburgs used Wawel as an army garrison.

Wawel Cathedral

Wawel 3 (012 429 33 27/www.wawel-krakow.pl). Tram 3, 6, 8, 10, 18, 40. **Open** *Oct-Apr 9am-4pm Mon-Sat; 12.30-4pm Sun. May-Sept 9am-5pm Mon-Sat; 12.30-5pm Sun.* **Admission** *with Cathedral Museum 10zł; 5zł reductions. No credit cards.* **Map** p93 B1 ❽

Krakow's key sight, along with St Mary's in the main square, is unmissable on three levels. Below, accessed through the crypt door on the left-hand side of the three-aisled nave, are lined the tombs of Poland's royal dynasties, military and literary heroes, the atmosphere suitably sombre. The nave, where royals were crowned, married and buried, lined with 18 chapels, is like a vast treasure chest of (mainly) Gothic and Renaissance styles. Follow the floor-tile arrows to find the standout Zygmunt Chapel halfway down the right-hand side. On the left-hand side is the doorway to the claustrophobic wooden staircase up the Zygmunt Tower – and its bell clapper you must touch with your left hand for good luck.

Eating & drinking

Hotel Poleski

NEW *Sandomierska 6 (012 260 54 05/www.hotelpoleski.pl). Tram 18, 19, 22.* **Open** *noon-11pm daily.* **Restaurant.** **Map** p93 A2 ❾

This newly opened hotel, its entrance hidden away near Manggha opposite Wawel, provides a rare example of a restaurant using the Vistula for backdrop. On the first floor, a window running its whole length, dine on quality versions of Polish classics. There's a summer bar terrace higher up too.

Kawiarnia pod Baszta

Wawel 3 (012 422 75 28/www.wawel-krakow.pl). Tram 3, 6, 8, 10, 18, 40. **Open** *Nov-Mar 9am-5pm daily. Apr-June, Sept, Oct 9am-5pm Mon-Fri; 9am-6pm Sat, Sun. July, Aug 8.15am-6pm daily.* **Café-restaurant.** **Map** p93 B1 ❿

The terrace café and restaurant in the main building of Wawel's outer courtyard provides breakfasts of French toast or omelette, four soups, a kids' menu, lunches such as pork chops or grilled salmon, plus the standard fruit cakes and ice-creams. Prices, for the location, are very reasonable.

Klub Panorama

Jubilat, Zwierzyniecka 50 (012 422 28 14/www.panoramaklub.eu). Tram 1, 2 6. **Open** *11am-10pm daily.* **Bar-restaurant.** **Map** p93 A1 ⓫

A real find, this. Through the riverfront door of the Jubilat shopping centre you press for the lift to take you to the top floor. Walk through a bar-disco area to a two-space terrace, one overlooking Wawel and the river, the other facing the green expanse to the west. Standard meals at standard prices, including a 15zł daily special, are provided, along with a choice of 30 cocktails for sunset and beyond.

Wawel Castle

Manggha

Konopnickiej 26 (012 267 27 03/www.
manggha.krakow.pl). Tram 18, 19, 22.
Open 10am-6pm Tue-Sun. **Café-**
restaurant. **Map** p93 A2 ⑫

The best museum eaterie in town is
this sushi bar and café, its terrace on
the Vistula. Along with 29zł sushi sets
(26zł for vegetarians), teriyaki, miso
soup and individual sushi snacks, you
can sip an Asaki or Sapporo beer, perhaps with a ginjou sake chaser.

Mauretania

Bulwar Kurlandzki (mobile 0692 383
661/www.mauretania.biz). Tram 3, 6,
8, 10, 40. **Open** 11am-last guest daily.
Bar-restaurant. **Map** p93 C4 ⑬

Offering better options for lunch or dinner than the floating venues nearer to
the Wawel complex, the Mauretania
can provide golden sole or veal in gor-
gonzola sauce in a below-deck dining
room lined with retro drink ads and
postcards of old Krakow. Afterwards,
choose among nine mojitos, 15 long
drinks and 20 short ones (or Ukrainian
wine!) from your panoramic seat on the
upper deck.

Restauracja na Wawel

Wawel 3 (012 422 75 28/www.wawel-
krakow.pl). Tram 3, 6, 8, 10, 18, 40.
Open *Nov-Mar* 9am-4pm daily. *Apr-*
June, Sept, Oct 9am-5pm Mon-Fri;
9am-6pm Sat, Sun. *July, Aug* 8.15am-
6pm daily. **Bar-restaurant**. **Map**
p93 B1 ⑭

While most visitors plot up at the busy
Kawiarnia in main courtyard, locals
head round the building to this large
terrace restaurant, for Lithuanian
meatballs, blini or duck in Grand
Marnier sauce. There's a café too, with
an expansive terrace overlooking the
Vistula and southern Krakow beyond.

Victoria Pub

Powiśle (012 626 81 40). Tram 1, 2,
6. **Open** 11am-last guest daily. **Bar-**
restaurant. No credit cards. **Map**
p93 A1 ⑮

The reward for your hard morning's
sightseeing around Wawel is this floating bar on the embankment just below,
serving Okocim beer, ice-creams and
snacks. You've two decks to choose
from, depending on the weather, and
the option of late drinking if required.

Hotel Poleski p96

St Joseph's Church p104

Podgórze & the South

From 1945 to recent times, the only foreigners of note who visited this neglected enclave across the Vistula from Kazimierz were Australian author Thomas Keneally and filmmaker Steven Spielberg. Each was drawn to the intact remains of the tragedy that took place here, when Podgórze contained the Jewish Ghetto set up by the Nazis in 1941. Unspeakable horrors occurred, most notably the massacre on the main square, then plac Zgody, in March 1943, and the forced marches to the nearby camp at **Płaszów** or out to Auschwitz.

What Keneally found and Spielberg followed up on was the legend of one man whose deeds came to signify the good in man whatever the odds: **Schindler**. His factory here in Podgórze is now an essential stop on the well-beaten themed tourist trail. Other sites include the square itself, renamed **plac Bohaterów Getta** ('Victims of the Ghetto') and housing an art installation related to the deportations; on one corner, the **Eagle Pharmacy**; remnants of the **Ghetto Wall**; and the bleak Płaszów site itself.

The success of Spielberg's film helped promote and revive the Jewish quarter of Kazimierz through the 1990s. Ten years later, the fashion for setting up trendy spots in gloomy localities with a war-related legacy crossed the river: the influential **Drukarnia**

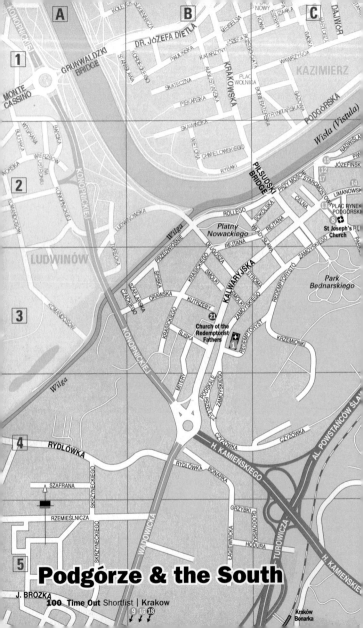

Podgórze & the South

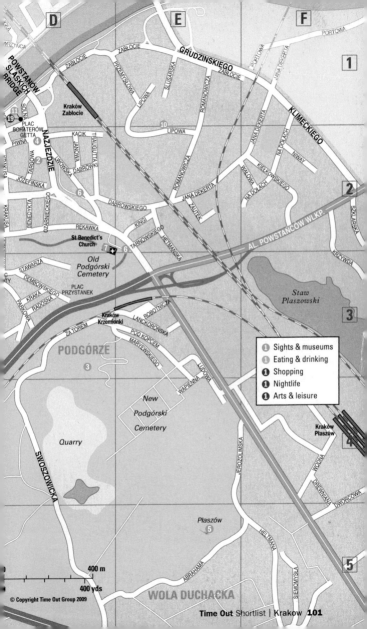

D · E · F

1

PORTOWA

GRUDZINSKIEGO

ZABŁOCIE

ZABŁOCIE

ZABŁOCIE

JANA DEKERTA

PORTOWA

KLIMECKIEGO

POWSTANCOW SLASKICH BRIDGE

SIODŁA

11
19

PLAC BOHATERÓW GETTA

Kraków Zabłocie

BRZANOWSKA

SLUSARSKA

IGDOWA

ROMANOWICZA

LIPOWA

10

JANA DEKERTA

NA DOŁACH

NIWY

4

KACIK

TRAUGUTTA

WIŁONA

KIELKOWSKIEGO

NA DOŁACH

PIWNA

NAZJEZDZIE

TARGOWA

JANOWA

LITOWSKA

DABROWKI

2

2

JÓZEFIŃSKA

6

DĄBROWSKIEGO

JANA DEKERTA

ZAŁTEK

AL. POWSTANCÓW WLKP.

SZKLARSKA

2

BENEDYKTA

CZARNIECKIEGO

RĘKAWKA

KINGI

TARNOWSKIEGO

HETMAŃSKA

KRZYWDA

KRAKUSA

St Benedict's Church

6

Old Podgórski Cemetery

Staw Płaszowski

3

STAWARZA

DEMBOWSKIEGO

KRAKA

RADOSNA

PABIOWA

PLAC PRZYSTANEK

Kraków Krzemionki

LANCKORONSKA

ROBOTNICZA

3

PODGÓRZE

ZA TOREM

POD KOPCEM

MARIEWSKIEGO

LIPOWA

3

New Podgórski Cemetery

WAPIENNA

	Sights & museums
1	Eating & drinking
1	Shopping
1	Nightlife
1	Arts & leisure

Quarry

SWOSZOWICKA

JEROZOLIMSKA

Kraków Płaszów

WODNA

DREWNIANA

DWORCOWA

4

Płaszów

5

HETMANA

5

400 m

400 yds

© Copyright Time Out Group 2009

ABRAHAMA

SIEMOMYSLA

WOLA DUCHACKA

bar moved premises to a riverside corner of Podgórze. Six months later, Med taperia **Cava** opened. Galleries set up in the streets leading off the market square, overshadowed by **St Joseph's Church**, a neighbourhood film director Roman Polanski would remember from his childhood.

Almost improbably, a luxury business hotel, the Qubus, was recently opened, set right by the old Ghetto square. Guests can relax in the panoramic rooftop pool and jacuzzi, seven storeys above the site of so much bloodshed and horror. The proposed waterfront development along the Vistula will only help bring more business to this once forgotten neighbourhood.

Sights & museums

Church of the Redemptorist Fathers

Zamoyskiego 56 (no phone). Tram 8, 10, 11, 23, 40. **Open** for services. **Admission** free. **Map** p100 B3 ❶
Designed by Jan Sas-Zubrzycki, also responsible for the similar St Joseph's built at the same time nearby, this Gothic-style parish church features later mosaics by Stanisław Jakubczyk and original stained glass by Stanisław Żeleński. Worth a detour.

Eagle Pharmacy

Pl Bohaterów Getta 18 (012 656 56 25). Tram 3, 6, 9, 13, 23, 24. **Open** *Nov-Mar* 10am-2pm Mon; 9am-4pm Tue-Thur, Sat; 10am-5pm Fri. *Apr-Oct* 10am-2pm Mon; 9.30am-5pm Tue-Sun. **Closed** 1st Tue/mth. **Admission** 5zł; 3zł reductions. Free Mon. **Map** p101 D2 ❷
The key site on the Schindler trail, this wartime pharmacy run by Tadeusz Pankiewicz was a meeting point and life-saving resource for Jewish families of the Ghetto – Pankiewicz was the only gentile allowed to run a business here. While the entrance still resembles a traditional apothecary, three rooms have been converted into a museum.

Letters, maps and film document the Ghetto years, the descriptions of climbing through the sewers to an uncertain fate truly moving. Post-war letters of appreciation from around the world to the hero chemist are kept in the back of the main room.

Krak's Mound

Krzemionki. Tram 3, 6, 9, 13, 23, 24. **Admission** free. **Map** p101 D3 ❸
Erected in the same era as Wanda's Mound near Nowa Huta, this prehistoric hillock is named after the city's first ruler. It's a popular spot for weekend hikes and picnics. See box p108.

Plac Bohaterów Getta

Pl Bohaterów Getta. Tram 3, 6, 9, 13, 23, 24. **Map** p101 D2 ❹
The former plac Zgody was the site of round-ups, deportations and a two-day massacre under the Nazi regime. Since renamed 'Square of the Victims of the Ghetto', this bleak, grey expanse of tramlines and new businesses now features a permanent installation by Piotr Lewicki and Kazimierz Łatak, opened in 2005. *Nowy Plac Zgody* comprises 70 chairs dotted around the square, the architects focusing on the mundane detail of abandoned furniture to bring out the horror of families being marched off never to return. The Eagle Pharmacy stands in the far corner.

Płaszów

Tram 3, 6, 9, 13, 23, 24. **Map** p101 D/E 4/5 ❺
Between the main roads of Wielicka, Kamieńskiego and Powstańców Śląskich is an expanse of hilly land steeped in blood: Płaszów. This was the site of the forced labour camp at the Liban Quarry. Walk up from the drive-in McDonald's on Wielicka, near the Dworcowa tram stop, and you come to a path, where Jerozolimska turns into Wiktora Heltmana. At Heltmana 22 stands a house, still occupied but its legacy unrecognised – here lived notorious camp commandant Amon Göth, played by Ralph Fiennes in Spielberg's *Schindler's List*. The quarry is beyond, the machinery visible through the

Schindler's legacy

Reformed Nazi entrepreneur revives Podgórze.

It was a story told by Holocaust survivor Poldek Pfefferberg to Australian author Thomas Keneally, chanced upon in Pfefferberg's leather-goods store in Beverly Hills. Keneally had gone in for a briefcase and came out persuaded that an ex-Nazi factory owner, Oskar Schindler, would make a cracking idea for a novel. Pfefferberg, one of 1,098 Jews saved by Schindler, had brought his papers from Europe. This was not the first Hollywood writer he had buttonholed.

With Pfefferberg's help, Keneally toured Podgórze and found the sites and survivors he spoke of. *Schindler's Ark*, a literary rework of (very) personal history, became a bestseller; Steven Spielberg made the film version. All three parties were at the night it won seven Oscars.

The Oskar of lore was no angel, which is what drew Keneally to him. A Sudeten German from Moravia, he had taken over a factory in newly occupied Poland. He made enamel goods, and soon, weapons – Jewish employees were cheap labour. Seeing the beatings around the Ghetto, Oskar began to bypass Nazi law, often at great risk, to help and save them. This womanising, brandy-swigging boss partied hard with loathsome fellow Nazis – not least Amon Göth, sadistic commandant of the notorious Płaszów camp nearby.

After Soviet liberation, Oskar and his equally heroic wife Emilie fled. Persecuted by Germans in Germany and Argentina, they never settled. Business ventures failed. Oskar visited Israel, where he was feted and, in 1974, buried. Emilie died in Berlin in 2001.

By then Schindler was a household name. Tourists ventured from the Old Town to find the film's locations: the courtyard between Józefa and Meiselsa in Kazimierz; the Ghetto in Podgórze; the factory (p104); Płaszów (p102), and, ultimately, Auschwitz (p125).

Tours were laid on and maps put on plac Bohaterów Getta. Yet there isn't that much to see. The factory is closed, binbags on its windows. Two bits of the Ghetto wall remain. Płaszów is untended.

The idea to revive the factory comes with its recent use as a concert venue and rumour of a Museum of Contemporary Art. Most of all, Jewish culture is being reinvigorated, with a major summer festival (p81), new museums and restaurants. Neither Schindler nor Spielberg is directly responsible – but both played a role in Krakow's revival.

KRAKOW BY AREA

fence in the film set. A large sign requests that those entering show reverence. A path up from Heltmana 40C leads to two plaques and a towering monument by Witold Cęckiewicz of five bowed heads on slender bodies, erected to Płaszów's victims in 1964. A gap runs all the way along where their hearts would have been.

Remnants of the Ghetto Wall

Limanowskiego 62 & Lwowska 25-29. Tram 3, 6, 9, 13, 24. **Map** p101 D2 & E2 ⑥

Its top carved into half-moon shapes similar to Jewish gravestones, the wall of the Ghetto once ran between the main market square and plac Zgody. All that remains are these two sections, most visibly the 12m-long stretch on Lwowska marked with a plaque in Polish and Yiddish.

St Benedict's Church

A Stawarza (no phone). Tram 3, 6, 9, 13, 24. **Open** 1st Tue after Easter. **Map** p101 D2 ⑦

Although this tiny church tucked in behind the trees only opens once a year to tourists, St Benedict's is of sufficient historical interest to merit a perusal from the outside. First built by Benedictine monks from Tyniec in AD 1,000, this church was converted into its more conventional, single-nave form from the previous rotunda shape. It was then added to over the centuries since. The view from the nearby cliff edge of Lasota Hill is outstanding.

St Joseph's Church

Zamoyskiego 2 (no phone). Tram 3, 6, 9, 13, 24. **Open** for services. **Admission** free. **Map** p100 C2 ⑧

Church architect Jan Sas-Zubrzycki, also responsible for the nearby Church of the Redemptorist Fathers at the same time, recreated this neo-Gothic landmark from a 19th-century classical temple that stood here before. When opened, in 1909, it rivalled St Mary's Basilica on the city skyline, a ploy by the ruling Habsburgs who exercised more control on this side of the river. It

still dominates Podgórze's market square. The interior may have something of the scale of St Mary's – but nothing like its colourful beauty.

Sanctuary of the Divine Mercy

Siostry Faustyny 3, Łagiewniki (012 252 33 11/www.sanktuarium-krakow.pl). Tram 8, 19. 23. **Open** for services. **Admission** free. **Map** p100 B5 ⑨

Inaugurated by Pope John Paul II in August 2002, this vast, bold, modern structure is one of Krakow's most radical architectural designs – Witold Cęckiewicz was the man responsible. It is set west of Podgórze, on the main road out to Łagiewniki, just past the Cinema City complex as you head south from town. Here stood a convent for fallen women; one, Sister Faustyna, was said to have witnessed a vision of Jesus. Her diary has been translated into many languages and this is a place of pilgrimage for her believers.

Schindler Factory

Lipowa 4 (no phone). Tram 3, 6, 9, 13, 24. **Map** p101 E1/2 ⑩

The latest word of Oskar Schindler's old factory complex, where 1,100 Jews were saved from extermination by making weapons for the Nazis, is that it will be a Museum of Contemporary Art. Other recent uses have included the staging of music for the Sacrum Profanum festival in 2008 and, of course, as a set for Spielberg's film – hence the sign 'Fabryka Oskara Schindlera – Emaila' over the gate. Before the museum opens, tourists will have to make do with peering through the fences. A plaque on the wall outside commemorates the three RAF South African airmen who were shot down here in 1944. See box p103.

Eating & drinking

After Work

Qubus Hotel, Nadwiślańska 6 (012 374 51 00/www.after-work.pl). Tram 3, 6, 9, 13, 24. **Open** 8pm-2am Tue-Sun. **Bar. Map** p101 D1 ⑪

Cava p107

Drukarnia

Unsurprisingly chic evening-only bar in Podgórze's business hotel, with live music Tuesdays and Thursdays, and cocktails (Blue Sky Delight, Absolut Ruby Red, Bols Melon, 34zl) six nights of the week. Tidy place to start the evening or bring a date – food includes salmon fillet and grilled sirloin of beef.

Cava

Nadwiślańska 1 (012 656 74 56/ www.cafecava.pl). Tram 3, 6, 8, 10. **Open** 8am-10pm Mon-Thur; 8am-midnight Fri; 9.30am-midnight Sat; 9.30am-9pm Sun. **Café-restaurant.** **Map** p100 C2 ⑫

Opened in 2007, this fashionable Med eaterie beside Drukarnia attracts the kind of young, professional local now moving into Podgórze. Breakfasts of imported cheeses and meats, lunches of superior baguettes and dinners of pasta, salads and snails prepared in several styles are served in a stylish interior, along with Latin-flavoured cocktails, southern European wines and the Spanish bubbly in question. Cava could have easily been cold and snobby – it's anything but.

Cesare

Rynek Podgórski 9 (012 263 80 30). **Open** 8am-10pm Mon-Sat; 9am-10pm Sun. **Restaurant.** **Map** p100 C2 ⑬

This prominent Italian on the main market square does a good job of serving quality mains (sea bass, chicken with raspberries), pastas and 20 kinds of pizza at fair prices. Desserts include towering fruit cocktails, stracciatelli ice-cream and waffles.

Delecta

Limanowskiego 11 (012 656 55 41). **Open** 11am-10pm Mon-Fri, Sun; 11am-11pm Fri, Sat. **Restaurant.** **Map** p100 C2 ⑭

By no means the best Italian in Krakow, and not even the best Italian in Podgórze, but the friendly Delecta allows you to tuck into seafood soup or risotto, one of 20 pizzas in two sizes, or mains such as sole in lemon sauce, in a pretty interior or outside on a quiet street in the evening sun. Dishes are

prepared in the busy, open kitchen and served by smiling, local staff. There are a dozen kinds of ciabatte too if you just need to fill a gap.

Drukarnia

Nadwiślańska 1 (012 656 65 60/www. drukarnia-podgorze.pl). Tram 3, 6, 8, 10. **Open** 9am-1am Mon-Thur, Sun; 9am-4am Fri, Sat. **Bar-venue.** **Map** p100 C2 ⑮

Jazz bar, locals' café and boho hangout, the Printing House would not look out of place by Canal St-Martin, Paris. But here it is, its scuffed tables overlooking the Vistula around sunset, its lived-in interior attracting barflies of all ages. Its move here from Kazimierz in 2007 raised eyebrows – now its bar has extended way back to cope with the crowds, and Bacardi is advertising all over it. There's still a magic feeling about crossing its threshold, under the original 'J Barucha' sign – all kinds of conversations and situations could spark up. Thoroughly recommended.

Magnifica

Farmona Business Hotel & Spa, Jugowicka 10C, Łagiewniki (012 252 70 70/www.magnifica.pl). Tram 8, 19. **Open** 10am-midnight daily. **Restaurant.** **Map** p100 B5 ⑯

Stand-out hotel restaurant set in the greenery of Łagiewniki, with a terrace overlooking lovely gardens. The modern European cuisine here is worth the tram or taxi down south (turn left from the main road at Sanctuary of the Divine Mercy Church). An inventive menu includes salmon soup with pumpernickel and marinated calf's liver; mains such as rabbit legs with green-pea purée, plus half-a-dozen choices for kids. There's a spa menu too, for healthy guests making use of the hotel's top-class treatments.

Rękawka

Brodzinskiego 4B (012 296 20 02). Tram 3, 6, 8, 10. **Open** 8am-10pm daily. **Café.** **Map** p100 C2 ⑰

Named after the festival held at nearby Krzemionki after Easter, this bohemian café set in a narrow, sunken

Pagan rites

Perhaps Krakow's most unusual and distinctive features are its mounds. These bizarre humps on the horizon first played a Stonehenge-like role in local history. Prehistoric, probably Celtic, man constructed the original hillocks, it is thought in order to coincide with pagan festivals. Krak's Mound (p102) in Podgórze was constructed around the same time as Wanda's Mound in what is now Nowa Huta. The sun rises exactly above Krak's on 1 November, the first day of the Celtic New Year; and above Wanda's on 1 May.

Following on from the pagan lead, 19th-century locals sought to assert their national identity under Habsburg rule by erecting a mound, Kościuszko (p117) named after the general who fought for Polish (and American) independence. Visit today and you'll also find a museum not only dedicated to the history of this phenomenon. Drawings of menfolk struggling with heavy wheelbarrows illustrate the construction of Kościuszko while early photos show couples in boaters and crinoline dresses enjoying a picnic around the base, still popular today. Further west than Kościuszko, another Polish hero, Józef Piłsudski, of World War I fame, was honoured with a mound (p130) afterwards. Subsequently, the Nazis and then the Soviets tried to raze it and thus destroy the idea of Polish independence. Inspired by the Solidarity movement of the 1980s, modern-day locals rebuilt their proud monument.

passageway has a somewhat literary feel to it. Comfortable armchairs sit beside a bookcase and an old typewriter. Peruvian, Hawaiian and Indian coffees are served and sold loose; apple, carrot, spinach or walnut cakes, salads and bruschette might accompany. Family visits are encouraged with the provision of colouring books and pens.

Arts & leisure

Cinema City
Zakopiańska 62, Łagiewniki (012 290 90 90/www.cinemacity.pl). Tram 8, 19, 23. **Open** according to programmme. **Map** p100 B5 ⑬
This contemporary ten-screen cinema complex south of town on the main road to Łagiewniki is a convivial venue to catch a movie. You'll find it ten minutes by tram from Podgórze on No.23.

Mile Stone
Qubus Hotel, Nadwiślańska 6 (012 374 51 00/www.mile-stone.pl). Tram 3, 6, 9, 13, 24. **Open** 7pm-2am Fri, Sat. **Map** p101 D1 ⑲
Half-decent live jazz is accommodated at weekends at this low-lit venue in the Qubus Hotel – don't expect anything radical or raucous but the riverside setting is nice. Free entry.

Starmach Gallery
Węgierska 5 (012 656 49 15/www. starmach.com.pl). Tram 3, 6, 9, 11, 23. **Open** 11am-6pm Mon-Fri. **Map** p100 C2 ⑳
Art historians Andrzej and Teresa Starmach, installed here since 1997, exhibit works by contemporary Polish artists and photographers at this former synagogue, a large and versatile space. Shows change every month.

Teranga Gallery
Kalwaryjska 48 (012 656 71 87). Tram 8, 10, 11. **Open** 10am-6pm Mon-Fri; 10am-2pm Sat. **Map** p100 B3 ㉑
Senegalese Papa Samba Ndiaye and his Polish wife Marżena opened this centre for African art and craft in 1999, showing and selling paintings, interior decoration and furniture.

plac Matejki

Kleparz & the North

Apart from its pair of produce markets, the closest ones to the city centre, **Kleparz** did not entice even locals to beat a path to its door – 'convents and brothels' was how one described it. This is changing with the reconfiguration of the railway station area on its doorstep. Along with the arrival of one of Poland's largest malls, **Galeria Krakowska**, business hotel **andel's** and cultural events on the relandscaped concourse, has come the recent opening of the **Krakow Opera** after years of delay.

Meanwhile, the dark streets north of the Old Town contain an odd scattering of museums – the chilling **Silesia House** is worth a visit – as well as the city's main cemetery, **Rakowicki**. If you can't be bothered to hop on a bus past the flyover to reach it, then a stroll around plac Matejki near the Old Town, its centrepiece **Grunwald Monument**, pretty **St Florian's Church** and noteworthy **Jarema** restaurant, should provide respite from tourist hordes.

Sights & museums

Botanical Garden
Kopernika 27, Wesoła (012 663 36 35/ www.ogrod.uj.edu.pl). Tram 4, 5, 10, 14, 15. **Open** *mid Sept-Mar* 9am-5pm daily. *Apr-mid Sept* 9am-7pm daily. **Admission** 5zł; 2zł reductions. No credit cards. **Map** p111 F5 ❶
The only site of note on Krakow's east side, these ten hectares of gardens and greenhouses contain some 6,000 varieties of plants, opened in the 1700s and renovated after the war. Don't miss the 500-year-old oak tree and impressive historic palm houses. The surrounding grounds feature modest Wesoła Palace,

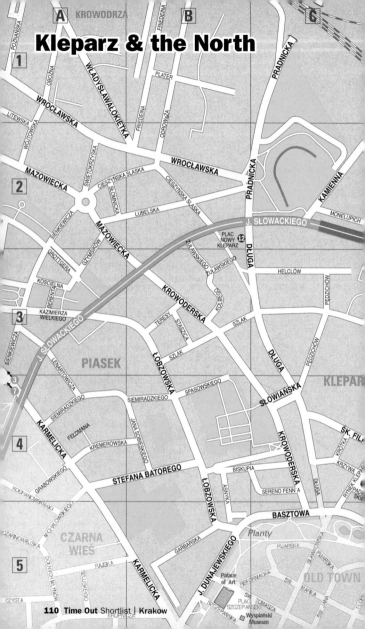

Kleparz & the North

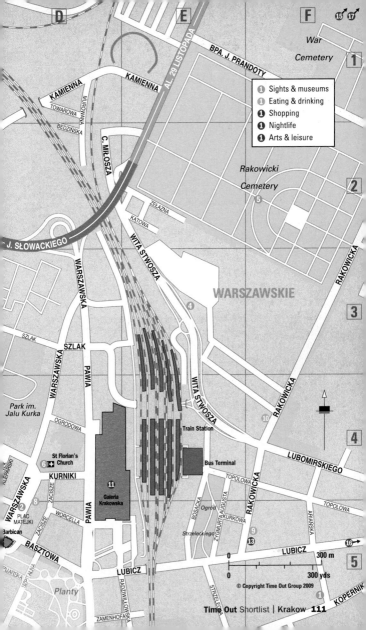

D **E** **F**

15↗ 17↗

War Cemetery

1

KAMIENNA

KAMIENNA

AL. 29 LISTOPADA

BPA. J. PRANDOTY

TOWAROWA

MUROWANA

BEDZINSKA

C. MILOSZA

Legend:
- ❶ Sights & museums
- ❶ Eating & drinking
- ❶ Shopping
- ❶ Nightlife
- ❶ Arts & leisure

Rakowicki Cemetery

❺

2

ZELAZNA

KATOWA

WITA STWOSZA

J. SŁOWACKIEGO

WARSZAWSKA

RAKOWICKA

WARSZAWSKIE

❹

3

SZLAK

WARSZAWSKA

SZLAK

PAWIA

WITA STWOSZA

RAKOWICKA

Park im. Jalu Kurka

OGRODOWA

❿

St Florian's Church
❻

KURNIKI

LUBOMIRSKIEGO

4

KLEPARSKI

ZACISZE

WARSZAWSKA

❷
❽

PLAC MATEJKI

Train Station

ZACISZE

Bus Terminal

PAWIA

WORCELLA

❶❶
Galeria Krakowska

TOPOLOWA

RAKOWICKA

TOPOLOWA

ARIANSKA

Barbican

BASZTOWA

BOSACKA

Ogród

ZYGMUNTA AUGUSTA

KURKOWA

❾

Strzeleckiego

❶❸

LUBICZ

16→

5

LUBICZ

0   300 m

0   300 yds

Planty

RADZIWILLOWSKA

ZAMENHOFA

STRZELECKA

© Copyright Time Out Group 2009

❶

KOPERNIK

while Kopernika contains four grand churches and university buildings.

Grunwald Monument

Pl Matejki. Tram 3, 4, 5, 7, 13, 14. **Map** p111 D4/5 ❷
Erected in 1910 on the day of the 500th anniversary of the historic triumph of the Poles over the Teutonic Knights, victorious leader King Jagiełło lording it over slain Ulrich von Jungingen, this formidable monument took the Nazis months to demolish in 1939-40. When it was eventually rebuilt, in the 1970s, it also incorporated 20th-century battle names around the plinth. Note that there is also a Grunwald Monument in Central Park, New York.

History of Photography Museum

Józefitów 16 (012 634 59 32/www. mhf.krakow.pl). Tram 4, 8, 13, 14, 24. **Open** 11am-6pm Wed-Fri; 10am-3.30pm Sat, Sun. **Admission** 5zł; 3zł reductions. No credit cards. **Map** p110 A3 ❸

Named after photo pioneer Walery Rzewuski, who lived along nearby Krupnicza in the 1800s, this obscure, modest but worthy first-floor museum contains Rzewuski-era equipment, magic lanterns, a camera obscura and early images of Krakow. Temporary photo exhibitions are also staged.

Home Army Museum

Wita Stwosza 12 (012 433 84 10/ www.muzeum-ak.krakow.pl). Tram 2, 11. **Open** 11am-5pm Tue-Fri. **Admission** 5zł. No credit cards. **Map** p111 E3 ❹
The Home Army (AK) was formed soon after the Nazi invasion of 1939, an underground Resistance whose brave operations are illustrated here with maps, medals, weapons and uniforms. The most renowned example of Polish armed uprising, in Warsaw in 1944, is outlined in depth in the corridor, while the walls in the long, dark main room are also lined with portraits of Polish heroes. The subject matter expands to

Rakowicki Cemetery

the fight for independence at various times in recent history. Documentation is detailed but sadly Polish-only; the boarded-up windows and overgrown grounds around the building could do with a tidy-up befitting the heroic sacrifice depicted within.

Rakowicki Cemetery

Rakowicka (no phone). Tram 2, 11/ bus 105, 114, 115, 129, 130, 139, 154, 159, 169, 179. **Open** *Nov-Feb* 7am-5pm daily. *Mar, Apr, Sept, Oct* 7am-6pm daily. *May-Aug* 7am-8pm daily. **Admission** free. **Map** p111 E/F 1/2 ❺

Poland's Père Lachaise was opened in 1803, the date over the main gate on Rakowicka – you can also enter from Al 29 Listopada, after the flyover north of the station. Residents include artists Jan Matejko and Józef Mehoffer at Nos.30 and 31 respectively – there's a map by the main entrance, where many graves are ornate. Some family ones – Heraszczenewskich, Lasockich, – are like small chapels. Pathways cut through greenery – it's a leafy stroll. Non-Poles include the Ukrainians who died at Dąbie in World War II, marked by a mound; Commonwealth, Soviet and Nazi soldiers slain in the same conflict are buried in the War Cemetery (same opening hours) across Prandoty.

St Florian's Church

Pl Matejki (no phone). Tram 3, 4, 5, 7, 13, 14. **Open** according to service. **Admission** free. **Map** p111 D4 ❻

The beginning of the Royal Route that led from Kleparz through the Old Town to Wawel, St Florian's was built in the late 12th century but fell victim to fire before its Baroque makeover in the 1700s. St Florian is the patron saint of chimneysweeps and firefighters.

Silesia House

Pomorska 2, Piasek (012 633 14 14/ www.mhk.pl). Tram 4, 8, 13, 14, 24. **Open** *Nov-Apr* 9am-4pm Tue, Thur-Sat, 2nd Sun/mth; 10am-5pm Wed. *May-Oct* 10am-5.30pm Tue-Sat, 2nd Sun/mth. **Admission** free. **Map** p110 A4 ❼

Red for go

December 2008 saw the unveiling of the most important cultural institution to open in Krakow for more than a century: **Krakow Opera** (p115).

Vienna has one, Budapest, Prague too, but for years Krakow Opera had to make do with performing at venues such as the Juliusz Słowacki Theatre until a new home was built close to the train station (and ornate Słowacki itself), on the site of the old, and equally ornate, Operetta Theatre. But there all comparisons end. This is no fin-de-siècle Baroque confection – the new Krakow Opera is striking, swish, contemporary, and red, bright red.

Architect Romuald Loegler, born locally in 1940, worked on Berlin's new city centre, and was responsible for the futuristic Łodz Philharmonic – it's no surprise that Krakow Opera is something entirely 21st century.

Within the scarlet exterior, its Great Stage features a computer-controlled acoustic ceiling and a movable orchestra pit. It was inaugurated with Krzysztof Penderecki's *The Devils of Loudun*. Upstairs are the Na Antresoli stage for smaller shows; the Chamber Stage; a restaurant; exhibition space, and a lecture hall.

Although Loegler's bright creation sticks out in this grey expanse of roundabouts and ring roads, by 2012 it will stand alongside the long-empty 'Skeletor' skyscraper, to be reconfigured as the Treimorfa Tower of offices, flats and perhaps a luxury hotel.

Grim but moving, behind a grey building on the corner of Pomorska and Królewska are the torture chambers used by the Gestapo. Four small cells scrawled with graffiti ('A message to Marylka – Witold Maskalik, 8.XII.44, 1300') can be visited once you ring the bell in the shabby courtyard. Upstairs is a permanent exhibition on the Resistance, in particular of the ŻOB Jewish unit. A sculpture of straining hands reaches out from the outer wall to bypassers on Pomorska.

Eating & drinking

Jarema
Pl Matejki (012 429 36 69/www. jarema.pl). Tram 3, 4, 5, 7, 13, 14. **Open** noon-midnight daily. **Restaurant. Map** p111 D4/5 ❽
For regional cuisine in relaxing surroundings, this rustic spot on plac Matejki makes for a pleasant evening in the company of (mainly) locals. Treats from eastern Poland and the former Polish territory of Lithuania include rare steak with cognac sauce, or berry sauces with pork and lamb dishes, followed by Lvov-style nougat for dessert. Traditional tunes tinkle out of a piano and lulling violins as waitresses in frilly costumes serve you the complimentary starter of lard and rye bread followed by the hefty main.

Sport Bar
Rakowicka 17 (012 623 77 69/www. sportbar.krakow.pl). Tram 2, 11. **Open** 11am-11pm Mon-Thur; 11am-midnight Fri; 1pm-midnight Sat, Sun. **Bar. Map** p111 F5 ❾
Krakow's only sports bar is set in a bare-brick cellar decked out with souvenirs of Krakow Tigers American football team and World Cup match tickets for Poland. A lively, regular young crowd is attracted by the promise of happy-hour beer from 6pm on weekdays.

Zbrojownia
Rakowicka 22 (012 613 14 86). Tram 2, 11. **Open** 10am-10pm daily. **Restaurant. Map** p111 F4 ❿

The setting for this terrace restaurant is an army camp – hence the name, 'Arsenal'. Competitively priced Polish specialities (zander in almonds, sirloin in mushrooms) are served in leafy surroundings or a large, old-style interior – pear casserole with ice-cream rounds things off nicely.

Shopping

Galeria Krakowska
Pawia 5 (012 428 99 00/www.galeria-krakowska.pl). Tram 2, 3, 5, 7, 10, 13, 19, 24. **Open** 9am-10pm Mon-Sat; 10am-9pm Sun. **Map** p111 D4/5 ⓫
Opened for Christmas 2006, this may not be Poland's biggest mall but it's certainly the most impressive. Some of the big names among the 270 stores were then new to Poland – Nike, Zara, Hilfiger, Swatch, adidas, they're all here. The steel-and-glass, three-level building links the train station with the Old Town – you may find yourself stepping off a train and into Benetton.

Nowy Kleparz
Pl Nowy Kleparz (no phone/http:// kleparz.krakow.pl). Tram 2, 3, 5, 7, 19. **Open** 6am-dusk Mon-Sat. **Map** p110 B2 ⓬
The newer of the two local markets, the partly covered Nowy Kleparz carries more jumpers, coats and clothing than its older counterpart three tramstops nearer to the city centre down Długa. Flowers stalls stretch out right along the length of the Długa side. Outside, cherubic ladies sell *oscypek* cheese snacks from Zakopane.

Nunc
Rakowicka 11 (012 421 99 55/www. nuncfashion.com). Tram 2, 11. **Open** noon-6pm Mon-Fri. **Map** p111 F5 ⓭
Born in Krakow in 1982, Dominika Nowak gave her first fashion show 16 years later – and, after also gaining experience working in Paris, this is her first boutique. Among Nowak's original, funky creations for shoes, clothes and accessories are her signature high heels and items showing hairy, spotty animal hides.

Jarema

Stary Kleparz

Krowodorska (012 634 15 32). Tram 3, 5, 7, 19. **Open** 6am-dusk Mon-Sat. **Map** p110 C4 ⑭

There has been a market just off plac Matejki since medieval times. Today's 70-stall venue contains fish shops, bakers and produce outlets under cover; peasants come from the country to sell cream cheese, dried fruits and dark local *węgierka* plums in the open air.

Arts & leisure

Aqua Park

Dobrego Pasterza 126 (012 616 31 90/www.ParkWodny.pl). Bus 125, 128, 132, 138, 139, 142, 152, 159, 172, 501. **Open** 8am-10pm daily. **Admission** *1hr* 12zł-21zł; 10zł-18zł reductions, under-7s. *2hrs* 29zł-31zł; 24zł-27zł reductions, under-7s. *Day* 40zł-46zł; 32zł-37zł reductions, under-7s. Under-3s free. **Map** p111 F1 ⑮

Krakow's water park an easy bus ride north-east from the Old Town features a dizzying array of tubes, shutes, slides and rope walks – not to mention the climbing walls whose safety net is the water below. Also popular with kids is the warm-water river rush; and with grown-ups, the salt-water jacuzzi and sauna. Tickets are cheapest first thing in the day.

Krakow Opera

NEW *Lubicz 48 (012 296 62 68/www. opera.krakow.pl). Tram 4, 5, 10, 14, 15.* **Open** according to programmme. **Map** p111 F4 ⑯

Opened in December 2008, this controversial crimson building stages opera, ballet and concerts. See box p113.

Multikino

Dobrego Pasterza 128 (012 617 63 99/www.multikino.pl). Bus 125, 128, 132, 138, 139, 142, 152, 159, 172, 501. **Open** according to programmme. **Map** p111 F4 ⑰

In the same complex as the Aqua Park, this multiplex stages all-nighters to a young crowd.

KRAKOW BY AREA

Bagatela Theatre p124

Czarna Wieś & the West

Just west of the Old Town thrives a revived student quarter dotted with new bars and restaurants. **Enso**, **Da Cesare** and **Avanti** all warrant the (maximum) ten-minute walk from the main market square. Just beyond is the outer ring road and the hub of the **National Museum** and the landmark Cracovia Hotel – and beyond that stretches a vast expanse of green easily accessible by tram or bus; **Park Jordana** and the **Błonia Meadow**. Krakow's own Bois de Boulogne is pleasingly featureless – you can see the **Kościuszko Mound** from way in the distance.

Further out towards the city limits, attractions include **Tyniec Abbey**, **Las Wolski** woods containing **Krakow Zoo**, and the **Bielany Hermitage**. See p125.

South of the student quarter are the districts of **Nowy Świat** and, tucked in by the river, **Salwator**. At the terminus of three tram routes, hilly and village-like, with its own market, Salwator is now a desirable residency, the bohemian atmosphere of its 19th-century heyday giving way to new builds.

Sights & museums

Błonia Meadow/ Park Jordana

Al 3 Maja, Czarna Wieś. Tram 15, 18. **Map** p118 C3 ❶
Krakow's most accessible green space, a 15-minute walk or short tram ride from the Old Town, is divided into two

areas: the enclosed Park Jordana, with a boating lake, sports courts and a recently installed skate park; and the adjoining open meadow of Błonia, lined with cycle paths and little else. Here John Paul II spoke to the largest gathering of Poles in history in 2002, his last public appearance on home soil.

Carmelite Church

Karmelicka 19 (012 632 67 52). **Open** 9.30am-4.30pm daily. **Admission** free. **Map** p119 F1 ②

Quite an odd history is attached to this church, a Baroque re-creation of the original built here in the 11th century. Duke Władysław Herman cured a hideous rash on his leg with sand found on this spot – the votive church he erected is still also known as the Church on the Sand. Its gleaming sacristy, brightened up in a recent overhaul, is worth a look.

Józef Mehoffer House

Krupnicza 26 (012 370 81 88/www. muzeum.krakow.pl). Tram 8, 15. **Open** 10am-6pm Tue-Sat; 10am-4pm Sun. **Admission** 6zł; 4zł reductions. Free Sun. **Map** p119 E/F 1/2 ③

This one of Krakow's nicest visits, a house with all its 19th-century family furnishings, plus a garden and café. For those interested in the Młoda Polska movement, it offers an entertaining insight into its key figures. First, artist and architect Stanisław Wyspiański was born here in 1869; his ageing contemporary Mehoffer took it over in 1932. His son Zbigniew converted it into a museum after the war. Look out for the replica of a stained-glass window by Wyspiański and Mehoffer senior, the *Life of Virgin Mary*; and, in room 13, a set of Japanese woodprints in what was Mehoffer's studio. See p37.

Kościuszko Mound

Al Waszyngtona, Zwierzyniec (012 425 11 16/www.kopieckosciuszko.pl). Bus 100, 101. **Open** 9.30am-dusk daily. **Admission** *Spring, autumn, winter* 7zł; 5zł reductions. *Summer Fri-Sun, hols* 8zł; 5zł reductions. Free 24 Mar, 3 May, 11 Nov. **Map** p118 A5 ④

June bridesmaids

Football's Euro Championships, the world's third biggest sports event after the Olympics and the World Cup, is coming to Poland in June 2012 – but not Krakow.

Easily the nation's leading tourist destination, Krakow has more hotel rooms than anywhere outside of Warsaw (and far better restaurants) and hosts the country's most successful football club in recent seasons. Even Pope John Paul II played as goalkeeper in his home town.

And yet the four Polish stadia sharing the honour with a quartet of counterparts in the Ukraine (tourism? hotels?) will be in Warsaw, Poznań, Gdańsk and Wrocław. None have yet been built. Warsaw's is the site of the biggest flea market in Eastern Europe, no idle boast. Governing body UEFA has threatened to move 2012 elsewhere – poor infrastructure would be reason enough. Still Krakow, like John Paul II in his day, is only a mere reserve.

The four winning bidders bent over backwards to present the most impressive prospectus to a national football authority later punished for corruption. Tourist-swamped Krakow practically waited to be asked. No-one did.

With building work going ahead at all four sites, UEFA threats aside, Krakow will watch Euro 2012 over its neighbour's fence. The 34,000-capacity Wisła stadium is being overhauled anyway – work on the VIP West Stand finishes in 2010. What about the World Cup in 2026?

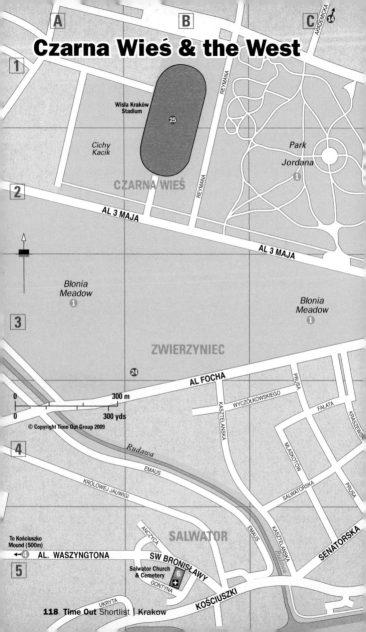

Czarna Wieś & the West

A **B** **C**

1

AKADEMICKA

14

Wisła Kraków
Stadium

25

Cichy
Kacik

REYMANA

Park
Jordana

1

2 CZARNA WIEŚ

AL 3 MAJA

REYMANA

AL 3 MAJA

Błonia
Meadow
1

3 ZWIERZYNIEC

Błonia
Meadow
1

24

AL FOCHA

PRUSA

WYCZÓŁKOWSKIEGO

KASZTELAŃSKA

FALATA

KRASZEWSKI

0 ———— 300 m

0 ———— 300 yds

© Copyright Time Out Group 2009

MASKOTÓW

Rudawa

4

EMAUS

SALWATORSKA

PRUSA

KRÓLOWEJ JAUWIGI

EMAUS

KASZTELAŃSKA

SENATORSKA

ANCZYCA

SALWATOR

Rudawa

To Kościuszko
Mound (500m)

5 ← 4 AL. WASZYNGTONA

SW BRONISŁAWY

Salwator Church
& Cemetery 6

GONTYNA

UKRYTA

KOŚCIUSZKI

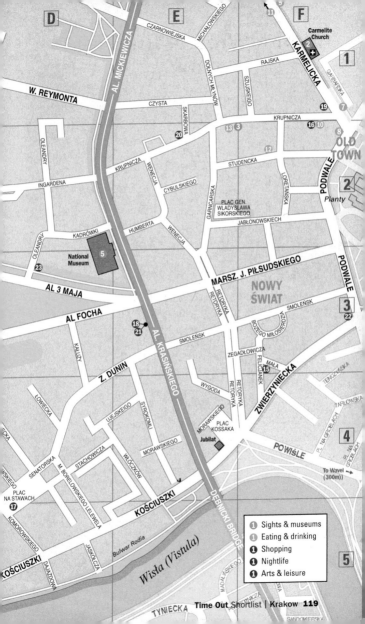

Da Cesare

Of Krakow's handful of mounds, either original prehistoric man-made hillocks or more recent erections to national heroes, the one to General Tadeusz Kościuszko is the most accessible. Surrounded by a waxworks museum (more national heroes) and a terrace café, the mound is scaled by a spiral staircase leading to a fine view. Behind the café, a museum details the history of mounds themselves, and the life of the man who fought for Polish and American independence. See box p108.

National Museum

Al 3 Maja 1, Czarna Wieś (012 295 55 00/www.muzeum.krakow.pl). Tram 15, 18. **Open** *10am-6pm Tue-Sat; 10am-4pm Sun. 1st Fri/mth 10am-8pm.* **Admission** *Day ticket 20zł; 10zł reductions. Free Sun. Gallery of 20th-century Polish Art 10zł; 5zł reductions. Arms & Colours of Poland/Gallery of Decorative Arts 6zł; 3zł reductions.* **Map** p119 D2/3 ⑤
The main branch of Krakow's National Museum is set in an institutional building where the outer ring road meets the main roads heading west – you could easily ignore it. Don't, for inside on the top floor is the finest collection of modern Polish art, featuring pieces from the fin-de-siècle Młoda Polska movement (Olga Boznańska, Wyspiański); the post-war Krakow Group; and set designer Tadeusz Kantor. Below, the Gallery of Decorative Arts includes jewellery, textiles and ceramics, Polish and European; the permanent display of military artefacts and uniforms on the ground floor, 'Arms & Colours of Poland', is closed for 2009. See p37.

Salwator Church & Cemetery

Św Bronisławy/Al Waszyngtona, Salwator (no phone). Bus 100, 101/tram 1, 2, 6. **Open** *varies.* **Admission** *free.* **Map** p118 B5 ⑥
This steep then gentle walkway through Salwator's hilly enclave is lined by two landmarks: Salwator Church, part Romanesque, with 16th-century frescoes; and, further along, Salwator's elevated Cemetery, giving fine views for miles around. Bus Nos.100 and 101 terminating at the Kościuszko Mound pass them both.

Eating & drinking

Avanti

Karmelicka 7 (012 430 07 70/012 430 02 48/www.avanti.krakow.pl). Tram 4, 8, 13, 14, 24. **Open** *Restaurant* 3-11pm Mon-Fri; 1-11pm Sat, Sun. *Orangery* noon-10pm daily. **Restaurant. Map** p119 F1. **7**

One of the top Italians in town comprises a restaurant, a leafy orangery with winter garden and a café with summer garden. The menu in the orangery offers standard Polish choices along with veal in sundry tasty sauces, well executed pastas, and so on; look out for salmon and truffle paste on toast, and warm seafood salad, in the antipasti selection available at the restaurant.

CK Browar

Podwale 6-7 (012 429 25 05/www.ck browar.krakow.pl). Tram 8, 15. **Open** *Restaurant* noon-midnight Mon-Thur, Sun; noon-1am Fri, Sat. *Pub* 9am-2am Mon-Thur, Sun; 9am-4am Fri, Sat. **Pub-restaurant. Map** p119 F2 **8**

Sports bar, microbrewery, nightclub and restaurant, CK Browar is all things to all merry men, having expanded its remit of providing home-brewed varieties of beer (light, wheat, strong dark and ginger-spiced). Platters of ribs and pork knuckle fly out of the kitchen as lads and lassies chug back the mugs of ale – purpose may be somewhat one-track by the time the late-closing club gets going.

Cudowne Lata

Karmelicka 43 (012 632 27 29). Tram 4, 8, 13, 14, 24. **Open** 9am-midnight Mon-Sat; 11am-11pm Sun. **Bar.** No credit cards. **Map** p119 F1 **9**

This unsung bar and front garden popularised by local youth is a handy pit-stop when you tire of new venues in the student quarter trying to out-chic each other. There's nothing chic here, just a big tap of Paulaner Weißbier on the bar, a piano, a sewing machine and two rooms of busy chatter.

Da Cesare

Krupnicza 6 (012 421 00 87). Tram 8, 15. **Open** noon-10pm daily. **Restaurant. Map** p119 F2 **10**

The Cesare in question hails from Calabria, as do the spicy sausage, smoked bacon and other imports

Galeria Przyrody p122

(cheeses, shellfish) he uses to create authentic pizzas and pastas in a contemporary setting. Prices, given the quality and authenticity of the food on offer, are more than reasonable.

Enso

🆕 *Karmelicka 52 (012 633 65 20/ www.karmelicka52.com). Tram 4, 8, 13, 14, 24.* **Open** *Bar-restaurant* 9am-midnight Mon-Sat. *Club* 8pm-4am Fri, Sat. **Bar/restaurant-club. Map** p119 F1 ⑪

A prime indicator of how things are moving up in the locality is this newly opened, fashionable establishment where you can lunch on a choice of six salads, seafood risotto or a spaghetti puttanesca; choose from 40 cocktails (raspberry mojito, cherry margarita, Voo Voo with Wyborowa vodka); and, past the VIP rope, schmooze around a DJ basement with a consciously neat crowd at weekends.

Galeria Przyrody

Studencka 15 (mobile 0509 669 812/ www.galeriaprzyrody.pl). Tram 8, 15. **Open** 10am-10pm Mon-Thur, Sun; 10am-11pm Fri, Sat. **Café.** No credit cards. **Map** p119 F2 ⑫

Nature (*przyroda*) has a big hand in this basement café busy with students: juices include birch-tree, chokeberry and elderflower nectar; dried fruit features cranberries and large Israeli dates, and some of the 60 teas were grown on the slopes of Laos, Taiwan and Nepal. Greenery, tropical fish and colourful photographs of Asian scenes complete the picture.

Vega

Krupnicza 22 (012 430 08 46/www. vegarestauracja.com.pl). Tram 8, 15. **Open** 9am-9pm daily. **Restaurant. Map** p119 E2 ⑬

Krakow's two-venue chain of vegetarian eateries features the same budget menu of salads in two sizes, soups and stuffed peppers but this branch also offers a terrace on a quiet stretch of Studentia by the Józef Mehoffer House. Look out for the meat-free versions of Polish standards, *bigos* and so on.

Shopping

Lea market

J Lea/Nowowiejska, Nowa Wieś (no phone). Tram 4, 8, 13, 14, 24. **Open** *Winter, spring, autumn* 6am-6pm Mon-Sat. *Summer* 6am-7pm Mon-Sat. **Map** p118 C1 ⑭

This modest, little-known market carries the best quality produce in town, as well as cured meats, Lisiecka sausage and any number of preserves. Locals go for the orange-tinted saffron milk cap mushrooms in October, a local delicacy when fried in butter.

Massolit Books & Café

Felicjanek 4, Nowy Świat (012 432 41 50/www.massolit.com). Tram 1, 2, 6. **Open** 10am-8pm Mon-Thur, Sun; 10am-9pm Fri, Sat. **Map** p119 F3/4 ⑮

Managed by a friendly American pair and equally amicable young staff, this trove of old English-language books, clearly categorised with plenty of curiosities, is also used as a resource for local expats. As well as a café with current magazines at the front, there's a busy noticeboard for classifieds and kids' reading sessions on Sundays.

Naturalny Sklepik

Krupnicza 8 (012 422 96 83). Tram 8, 15. **Open** 9am-7pm Mon-Fri; 9am-2pm Sat. No credit cards. **Map** p119 F2 ⑯

Around the corner from Da Cesare (whose boss is one of several chefs who gives talks here) is a hidden garden courtyard with a cabin at the end of it, filled with exotic and often rare natural products: Naturalny Sklepik. With row upon row of wooden shelves heaving with bright merchandise and weird labels, it might be confusing, but the enthusiastic English-speaking staff are happy to guide you.

Salwator market

Pl na Stawach, Salwator (no phone). Tram 4, 8, 13, 14, 24. **Open** *Winter, spring, autumn* 6am-6pm Mon-Sat. *Summer* 6am-7pm Mon-Sat. **Map** p119 D4/5 ⑰

Locals swear by this market for range of products – not only fruit and veg but

Massolit Books & Café

soups (beetroot, *żurek*) sold in vodka bottles, assorted home-made preserves, sausages, herbs and spices plus rare seafood in the fish shop.

Nightlife

Kijów Club

Al Krasińskiego 34, Nowy Świat (012 422 36 77/www.kijowclub.pl). Tram 15, 18. **Open** 4pm-5am Thur-Sun; 4pm-1am Mon-Wed. **Map** p119 E3 ⑬

Although small, this sleek basement club in the same building as the Kijów Cinema attracts some of the best DJs Krakow has to offer. The visuals and music vids on the floor-tile screens can become a little disconcerting.

Arts & leisure

Bagatela Theatre

Karmelicka 6 (012 422 66 77/www. bagatela.pl). Tram 4, 8, 13, 14, 15, 24. **Open** *Ticket office* 9am-6pm Mon-Fri. **Map** p119 F1 ⑲

Named after Tadeusz Boy-Żeleński, itself a pseudonym, a critic, writer and major Młoda Polska figure, this theatre is the striking building at the junction of Karmelicka and Krupnicza. It was here that Roman Polanski made his stage debut. Today it shows Polish drama, musicals and light comedies.

Groteska Theatre

Skarbowa 2 (012 633 48 22/www. groteska.pl). Tram 8, 15. **Open** *Ticket office* 8am-noon, 3-5pm Mon-Fri. **Map** p119 E2 ⑳

Walk around the main market square in summer and you'll see puppet shows for kids – produced by Groteska, whose home is off Krupnicza. Re-enactments of popular fairy stories are programmed here throughout the year.

Kijów Cinema

Al Krasińskiego 34, Nowy Świat (012 433 00 33/www.kijowcentrum.pl). Tram 15, 18. **Open** according to programme. **Map** p119 E3 ㉑

In a landmark building designed by Witold Cęckiewicz, the Kijów contains the widest screen in town, and screen-ing rooms ranging from studio spaces to a near-1,000 seater – most convenient when the cinema becomes one of the main hosts of the annual Krakow Film Festival.

Krakow Philharmonic

Zwierzyniecką 1, Nowy Świat (012 429 13 45/www.filharmonia.krakow.pl). Tram 1, 2, 6. **Open** *Ticket office* 11am-2pm, 3-7pm Tue-Fri. **Map** p119 F3 ㉒

With its former chief conductor Tadeusz Strugała now in charge as general director, this renowned concert hall is in good hands. Honorary director is Krakow resident Nigel Kennedy. The Philharmonic itself moved into this neo-Baroque edifice, built before the war, in 1945.

Rotunda

Oleandry 1, Czarna Wieś (012 633 35 38/www.rotunda.pl). Tram 15, 18. **Open** *Ticket office* 10am-1pm, 4-7pm Mon-Fri. **Map** p119 D3 ㉓

A completely mixed bag of entertainment is staged here, a modest-sized venue near the National Museum – rock, pop, cabaret or folk dancing.

Salwator Juvenia

Na Błoniach 7, Salwator (012 421 49 85/http://juvenia.info). Tram 15, 18/ bus 134, 152, 192. **Open** according to programme. No credit cards. **Map** p118 B3 ㉔

Currently top of the ten-team domestic league, Krakow rugby team play at this modest ground on the Błonia Meadow. Matches take place at the weekend – check the site for details.

Wisła Kraków

Reymonta 22 (012 630 76 00/www. wisla-krakow.pl). Tram 15, 18. **Open** *Ticket office* 11am-6pm Mon-Fri; 10am-2pm Sat. **Map** p118 B1/2 ㉕

Poland's best football team of recent times (the current champions have won the league six times in ten years) play at this ground, a reserve venue for Euro 2012. There's a terrace bar by the gate on Reymonta. Rivals Cracovia play at a more modest ground on the other side of the Błonia Meadow. See box p117.

Bielany Hermitage p128

Trips

Auschwitz

No name conjures horror like
Auschwitz. One of the busiest
tour destinations from Krakow,
the most notorious of the Nazi
concentration camps lies 75km
(47 miles) west of the city, built
on to the little railway town of
Oświęcim – how Auschwitz is
marked on Polish maps, timetables
and road signs.

What was perpetrated here,
the mass murder of over a million
people in four-and-a-half years, in
two camps 3km (two miles) apart,
truly beggars belief. **Auschwitz
I**, opened in 1940, was at first a
labour camp, lined with wooden
huts, preserved as a museum
shortly after liberation in 1945.
Each hut is numbered and has
been dedicated to the victims from

certain nations – France, Hungary,
Yugoslavia, and so on. One gas
chamber remains, small but
horrifying, in a low-level building
beside which still stand the gallows
where camp commandant Rudolf
Höss was executed in 1947.

Auschwitz II-Birkenau,
opened in 1942, is a vast factory
complex dedicated to killing.
Here at any one time, up to 100,000
people occupied a 300-building site
of 175 hectares (430 acres), scraping
the depths of human misery to
survive on a day-by-day basis.
Here you see the watchtower and
railway lines, those images from
books and documentary films that
may have occupied your mind on
your journey here.

Most Krakow tour companies
include Auschwitz on their
itinerary. A tour allows you to see

both camps in one go – the public shuttle bus between the two doesn't run in winter. It's straightforward to take a bus from Krakow, then a local one to Auschwitz I (some Krakow ones go all the way), or a train; but the guided tour is worth the outlay. Guides tend to be sensitive and knowledgeable – it cannot be an easy job. Although local schoolchildren are taken round in groups, it is recommended that nobody under 14 should visit the camps.

It is also worth investing in the detailed guidebook (4zł), with maps on each cover flap, sold at the souvenir hut by the entrance. There's a café there too. A film shown in various languages in the main building was taken right after the Soviet liberation in 1945.

You start your journey where so many ended theirs: under the main gate and inscription, 'Arbeit macht frei'. Here, it is explained, a band would play each morning to send prisoners off to work. Drawings by Mieczysław Kościelniak describe the scene. This former pupil of Józef Mehoffer at the Academy of Fine Arts survived Auschwitz to help transform it as a museum. While interned he created 500 drawings, some on display here.

While taking you past the first set of wooden huts, the guide talks you through daily life in the camp: the deprivation, the brutality, the beatings. First you come to Hut 4, 'Extermination'. Inside is a model of Auschwitz II-Birkenau, canisters of Zyklon B pellets, the gas used to murder millions, and a display of three photographs, taken at great risk by an inmate, of corpses burning on a pyre. Alongside, in Hut 5, 'Material Evidence of Crimes', are displays of glasses, artificial legs, saucepans, Jewish

Auschwitz

Going underground

Salt proves to be a goldmine in Wieliczka.

Wieliczka is Poland's most popular tourist attraction. Every tour company in Krakow runs to this celebrated sight 15km (ten miles) south-east of the city. As entrance is by guided tour only (63zł/48zł), it's probably worth laying out the 100zł most charge for taking you there and back by coach, and getting you ahead of the slow queues outside. Once you're in, a huge lift packs in new arrivals 36 deep; you then shuffle round in stops and starts, waiting for those ahead to clear from one corridor or chamber.

So why do so many people want to go down a salt mine? Most are drawn here by the promise of **St Kinga's Chapel**, by far the most impressive of the scores of echoing spaces and statues carved entirely from salt. At 50 metres (164ft) long, accessed down a grand, slippery staircase and carpeted by a honeycomb floor, St Kinga's is breathtaking – altar, chandeliers, statues and bas-reliefs. It was carved in the early 1800s, although miners had been living underground and creating chapels long before. It has been a tourist attraction since Goethe's day. St Kinga's is also used as a banqueting hall and Mass is held her eevery Sunday.

St Kinga's is the highlight near the end of the two-hour tour. Much of the rest is disappointing – you'll be aghast when a light show starts up to Chopin music – but Wieliczka keeps the kids happy and quiet for most of a morning. As you go round you do learn about how the miners lived and worked; the lake at the very bottom is spooky, the rowboat unused since seven Austrian soldiers drowned a century ago. Those visiting today must be quite fit – there are lots of stairs to descend and corridors to traverse.

The most amazing thing is what you don't see. Wieliczka has 300km (186 miles) of galleries and 3,000 chambers – you will only visit 22 of them, and pass 2km (1.25 miles) of galleries.

prayer shawls, shoes, tins and two huge piles: one of human hair, another of suitcases, names and addresses scratched on the sides.

This may already be enough for some people – at any time you may step outside on to the path between huts – but worse follows at the end of the row, No.11, 'Death Block'. Here were the torture chambers and starvation cells, the kangaroo court and execution wall, now wreathed by flowers, candles and a flag in camp-uniform blue and white.

You may visit any of the huts, turned into national museums – Roma in No.13, Czechs and Slovaks in No.16, Hungarians in No.18. The guide then leads you, via the assembly square, into the gas chamber: a small, bare room with a little track leading out of it to an adjoining room of ovens.

The bus takes you on to Auschwitz-II Birkenau. There you climb the watchtower and train your eyes over row after row after row of stumps, way off into the distance, vestiges of the barracks that stood here before retreating Nazis destroyed them. Right at the far end were the crematoria. The rail line remains, as does the platform where new arrivals were immediately assessed for work duties or death. There are a few original barracks. You are taken to see one, its inhuman conditions described as accurately as you see around you. No one was meant to leave here alive.

Tour buses tend to ignore the village of Oświęcim 3km (two miles) away. If you're prepared to make your own way back to Krakow, it might be worth visiting the **Auschwitz Jewish Centre** near Oświęcim Castle by the river. Opened in 2000, it details the life of the Jewish community in the town before the Holocaust. You can also visit the untouched house of Szymon Kluger, the last Jewish resident of the community, who died before the museum opened.

Auschwitz

Oświęcim (033 844 00 00/www. auschwitz.org.pl). By tour/bus to Oświęcim. **Open** *Dec-Feb* 8am-3pm daily. *Mar, Nov* 8am-4pm daily. *Apr, Oct* 8am-5pm daily. *May, Sept* 8am-6pm daily. *June-Aug* 8am-7pm daily. **Closed** 1 Jan, Easter Sunday, 25 Dec. **Admission** free. *Guide* 35zł.

Most tours cost around 100zł-120zł from Krakow and include a bus there and back, transfer between the two camps and a guide. The public bus, one way Krakow-Oświęcim, is 10zł.

Auschwitz Jewish Centre

Pl Ks Jana Skarbka (033 844 70 02/ www.ajcf.org). Bus to Oświęcim. **Open** *Nov-Feb* 8.30am-6pm Mon-Fri, Sun. *Mar-Oct* 8.30am-8pm Mon-Fri, Sun. **Admission** *suggested donation* 6zł.

Las Wolski & Tyniec

West of Krakow, beyond the gentle, flat meadow of Błonia, stretches the open woodland of **Las Wolski**. Head to its main attraction, **Krakow Zoo**, at the terminus of the half-hourly No.134 bus that runs from the Cracovia Hotel facing the National Museum; by the main entrance is a map indicating hiking paths through the woods and sundry attractions, including the **Piłsudski Mound**. More city buses follow the river, allowing access to the **Bielany Hermitage** and the **U Ziyada** restaurant. Over the Vistula, at the city limits, the furthest attraction of **Tyniec Abbey** is best reached by boat from town in summer or by tour bus in winter.

Bielany Hermitage

Al Konarowa, Srebrna Góra, Las Wolski. Bus 109, 209, 229, 239. **Open** *Men* 8-11am, 3-4pm daily. *Women* 12 days/yr. **Admission** free.

Las Wolski

A bizarre sight this, and one only accessible to women on certain religious holidays (Whit Sunday, Easter etc). The strict Camadulensian order of monks has lived and worked here for centuries – you may see them quietly tending the gardens by their hilltop monastery. Bones of their predecessors are kept in the crypt. Male visitors are allowed in at half-hourly intervals.

Krakow Zoo

Las Wolski (012 425 35 51/www.zoo-krakow.pl). Bus 134. **Open** *Winter* 9am-3pm daily. *Spring, autumn* 9am-5pm daily. *Summer* 9am-7pm daily. **Admission** 14zł; 7zł reductions; free under-3s.

Rare species are the main attraction of this extensive breeding zoo, celebrating its 60th anniversary in 2009. Slap in the middle of Las Wolski woods, at the terminus of the No.134 bus, Krakow Zoo contains some 1,500 creatures representing 260 species. Ones to look out for are Przewalksi horses, no longer found in the Polish wilds, and, also bred in captivity, Andean condors, snow leopards and Chinese leopards.

Krakow Zoo

Visible from the café outside the main entrance is the elephant enclosure, home of local favourites Citta and Baby. There's a petting zoo too.

Piłsudski Mound

Las Wolski. Bus 134.

The most recent of Krakow's mounds to open – reopen, in fact – offers as good a view as Kościuszko's without its other visitor attractions. Named after Poland's World War I hero and erected when he died in 1937, the Piłsudski Mound was closed and almost razed by the Nazis and Soviets until Solidarity prompted its renovation and return to the fold in 2002.

Tyniec Abbey

Benedyktyńska 37, Tyniec (012 688 52 00). Bus 112. **Open** 7.30am-6.30pm daily. **Admission** varies.

The furthest sight you can visit without leaving Krakow itself, Tyniec is a popular destination for summer boat tours from town. Recitals take place at this 11th-century Benedictine abbey on balmy evenings – otherwise most are happy to gawp at the impressive setting high over the Vistula.

U Ziyada

Jodłowa 13, Zwierzyniec (012 429 71 05/www.uziyada.krakow.pl). Bus 109, 209, 229, 239, 249, 259, 269. **Open** 10am-10pm daily. **Restaurant.**
Well presented Kurdish cuisine would be reason enough to visit this attractive restaurant in the south-east corner of Las Wolski – but the building, Przegorzały, a grand riverside castle retreat for the Nazi officers in the war, is the real talking point here.

Willa Decjusza

28 Lipca 17A, Zwierzyniec (012 425 33 90/www.vd-restauracja.pl). Bus 102, 134, 152, 192. **Open** 10am-10pm daily. **Restaurant.**
The food may be excellent – it should be, main courses (scallops) running up to 139zł – but it's the setting that draws smart diners here, a beautifully renovated 16th-century villa in the park of the same name, by Las Wolski.

Essentials

Grand Hotel p135

Hotels

To say that the hotel stock here has improved in the last decade is an understatement. Before the mid 1990s there was almost nothing in terms of luxury or business lodging.

The noble monuments of Habsburg Krakow, the **Grand**, the **Pod Róza**, which in their day accommodated tsars, generals and famous composers, had been privatised but not yet reconfigured. The same was true of a slew of mid-range hotels, some not without their own architectural value – even today there's a stained-glass Wyspiański in the otherwise modest **Pollera**.

The revolution in local luxury lodging came with the **Likus** brothers' takeover of Pod Róza in 1994 and Jerzy **Donimirski** inheriting the **Pugatów Palace**

around the same time. Likus – designer Leszek, manager Tadeusz and financier Wiesław – made a success of Pod Róza then went on to even greater things, first at **Copernicus**, then at the **Hotel Stary**. While Donimirski was more concerned with the finery of dovetailing historic venues and contemporary comfort, the Likus Group went the whole nine yards by adding spas, pools and gyms.

The revamped Grand became Krakow's first five-star in 2004. On the main square itself, the **Pałac Bonerowksi** and the **Wentzl** had just set up to provide high-spec lodging too. In Kazimierz the **Rubinstein** and near Czarna Wieś the **Ostoya Palace** opened to similar high standard. Chains at either end of the scale, from **Radisson** and **Sheraton** to

Amadeus

Mikołajska 20 (012 429 60 70/ www.hotel-amadeus.pl). **ZZZ**.

As the name implies, this tasteful, four-star, 22-room a short walk from the main market square has been done out in the (Baroque) style of Mozart's day – although the original building, still showing the Odrowąż family coat of arms, dates from a century earlier. It was converted in 2000, and many a musician has stayed here since then. The fresco-lined cellar restaurant is a destination in its own right.

Copernicus

Kanonicza 16 (012 424 34 00/www. hotel.com.pl). **ZZZZ**.

Probably the best hotel conversion in the city, the sumptuous Copernicus is set on the cobbled street where Pope John Paul II served as bishop for 20 years, in a canon's house frequented by the famed astronomer himself. Almost

Novotel and **Ibis**, also set up. Hostels mushroomed.

Now Krakow has a hotel stock to rival that of Prague and Budapest, if not yet Vienna or Berlin. Its USPs are its historic buildings, its compact size (so that the main square or station is within easy reach) and its relatively attractive rates, particularly out of season. With more use being made of its waterfront, as recently exampled by the **Qubus** and the **Poleski**, Krakow has much to offer visitors at each end of the scale and in most areas of the city.

Hotels are busiest at Christmas and New Year. There is no major event or festival at other times to decrease availability dramatically.

For this guide, we have used the following rack-rate price categories for the cost of a double room:

Up to €100 Z
Up to €150 ZZ
Up to €200 ZZZ
Over €200 ZZZZ

SHORTLIST

For art-nouveau decor
- Pollera (p137)

For bargain beds
- Basztowa Guesthouse (p144)
- Kolory Bed & Breakfast (p141)

For boutique luxury
- Gródek (p135)
- Pugetów (p141)

For main-square location
- Dom Polonii (p135)
- Pałac Bonerowski (p137)
- Wentzl (p139)

For panoramic bathing
- Qubus Hotel (p143)

For presidential treatment
- Copernicus (see above)
- Grand Hotel (p135)

For spa breaks
- Farmona Business Hotel & Spa (p143)

ESSENTIALS

as inspired is the dovetailing of high-end customer demands with historic surroundings: a swimming pool and sauna luxuriate in medieval cellars; a 16th-century mural decorates a wall in room No.101, 17th-century decoration in room No. 108. There are 29 rooms in all. Guests – high-ranking politicians, film directors – also care to gather in the cigar lounge or on the rooftop terrace facing Wawel.

Dom Polonii

Rynek Główny 14 (012 428 04 60/ www.wspolnota-polska.krakow.pl). **Z**.
Three rooms right on Rynek Główny at knockdown prices, in a historic townhouse dating back to 1373 – no wonder 'Poland House' is booked out weeks in advance. But if you're planning a special trip (older visitors should be warned that the rooms are on the third floor and there's no lift), you won't find anywhere this comfortable this central at these prices.

Grand Hotel

Sławkowska 5-7 (012 421 72 55/ www.grand.pl). **ZZZZ**.

The proud date 1887 over the doorway, the liveried flunkies hopping to the sound of the bell, this is old-school hostelry of movie lore. Film crews, in fact, often shoot and or/lodge here. A century after the former Duke and Duchess Czartoryski (of Museum fame) sold their family home as a hotel, the complete renovation of the Grand, its 64 individually designed rooms, two cafés and restaurant, is indeed impressive – this was Krakow's first five-star hotel after the Changes. It may lack the space for a spa or pool but you'll be dining in a replica of the Mirror Hall restaurant where Joseph Conrad and the great cultural figures of the day would have convened.

Gródek

Na Gródku 4 (012 431 90 30/www. donimirski.com). **ZZZZ**.
It's comfort of the first order at the newest of historic boutique chain Donimirski's downtown hotels. As you pad around in your fluffy bathrobe, your feet warm from the heated bathroom floor, the medieval feel of the building around you is no coincidence

Gródek

Palac Bonerowski p137

– dating back to the turn of the last millennium, it was part of the nearby Dominican convent. Tiles and receptacles of the period discovered in this superb conversion are displayed under floods of natural light in the basement breakfast room and notable Cul-De-Sac restaurant. A common roof terrace is another fine feature. See box p145.

Hostel Flamingo

Szewska 4 (012 422 00 00/www. flamingo-hostel.com). **Z**.

You don't have to be a young hedonist on a budget to enjoy it here – but it helps. Five steps from the main square and barely a stagger from the nightspots lining this busy street, the Flamingo ('run by flamingos for flamingos') keeps backpackers happy with internet, cooking facilities, laundry, several washrooms and a spacious TV room overlooking Szewska. A mixed bag of events is laid on, from cultural tours to barhops. See box p140.

Pałac Bonerowski

Św Jana 1 (012 374 13 00/www. palacbonerowski.pl). **ZZZZ**.

Another quite masterly reconfiguration of a historic property into a serious five-star hotel, the Bonerowski has the bonus of a site overlooking the main market square. If you've landed one of six apartment suites here for the night, you've really arrived. There's a medieval pillar in the Presidential one. Eight rooms are also available, and non-guests can treat themselves to a high-class French or Italian meal at the Pod Winogronami restaurant.

Pod Róza

Floriańska 14 (012 424 33 00/www. hotel.com.pl). **ZZZZ**.

The most affordable hotel of the Likus Group's high-end clutch, the Pod Róza was the first that these enterprising brothers invested in. This was the blue-chip lodging of its day – Franz Liszt stayed here after a concert and Tsar Alexander after losing at Austerlitz. It took Likus ten years to rebuild and remodel it, opening in 2005. The suites may still accommodate opera stars and

movie moguls but half the rooms are limited by the dimensions of the building – there are also 'mansard' doubles under the roof. The 16th-century portal is a real gem, though, and it's worth breaking off a browse on Floriańska to visit the hotel's namesake restaurant.

Pollera

Szpitalna 30 (012 422 10 44/www. pollera.pl). **Z**.

One of the lesser-known stops on any Modernist tour of Krakow is this renovated 19th-century hotel at the train station end of the Old Town. Rooms may be quite chintzy, equipped in the standard fashion, but you're in a prime spot and for the winter months paying well less than 100 euros. As for the art nouveau, Wyspiański produced the stained-glass window on the staircase; the restaurant from the same period shows modernist touches that guests of ball-giving socialite Wanda Poller might have appreciated – her grandfather Kasper opened the hotel in 1834.

Senacki

Grodzka 51 (012 422 76 86/www. senacki.krakow.pl). **ZZ**.

This three-star near the landmark churches in the ecclesiastical quarter comprises 20 bright if occasionally boxy rooms, half of them twins, some of which (202-203, 302-304) overlook the Royal Route on Grodzka. It's another historic conversion but here the management has resisted the temptation to go chic or boutique – it's a fair rate for a fair room, with a decent restaurant thrown in for good measure.

Stary

Szczepańska 5 (012 384 08 08/www. hotel.com.pl). **ZZZZ**.

The Likus Group has pushed the boat out here, a luxurious 53-room five-star fitted in a townhouse from the 15th century. From the flat-sized suite to the singles on floors one to five, all is decked out with quality silks and marble, oriental carpets and exotic woods. Restaurant Trzy Rybki is reason alone to visit; swimmers bathe in warm water amid bare brickwork.

ESSENTIALS

OFF WHITE
BUSINESS AND LEISURE APARTMENTS

MINIMALIST IN DESIGN
EXCEPTIONAL IN SOPHISTICATION,
LOCATION AND PRESTIGE

Eight delightfully practical apartments and a singularly luxurious 150-square-metre penthouse make OFF WHITE *an extraordinarily desirable address for business travelers, families or tourists in Krakow's fashionable Kazimierz district.*

OFF WHITE – BUSINESS AND LEISURE APARTMENTS

ADDRESS: UL. KUPA 6, 31-057 KRAKÓW, POLAND

INFORMATION: INFO@OFFWHITE.PL

TELEPHONE.: +48 (12) 376 40 40

FAX: +48 (12) 376 40 50

WEB SITE: WWW.OFFWHITE.PL

Pod Róza p137

Trecius

Św Tomasza 18 (012 421 25 21/www. trecius.krakow.pl). **Z**.

Not too well known this place, but a lovely find nonetheless, and cheap with it. So close to the main square you can hear the hourly bugle call, this former residence of 16th-century court secretary Krzysztof Trecjusz contains six tidy doubles, equipped with heated bathroom floors, internet and satellite TV. All is set on the first floor of the building, the piano nobile. Breakfast isn't included in the price but you're a step away from café central.

Wentzl

Rynek Główny 19 (012 430 26 64/ www.wentzl.pl). **ZZZ**.

The management here may have only opened this 18-room hotel 208 years after the landmark restaurant (dated 1792), but the lush, bright, imaginative furnishings more than make up for any lack of guest-room heritage. And, as Wentzl is happy to point out, this is the only hotel completely on the main square. Rooms are lovely, tastefully and individually furnished, six on each of three floors – and you won't have to go too far to find a good restaurant.

Kazimierz & Stradom

Aparthotel Spatz

Miodowa 11 (012 357 20 13/www. spatz.pl). Tram 6, 8, 10. **ZZ**.

Opened in 1992, well before the Kazimierz revival, this comfortable, 28-unit house on a quiet street corner is well positioned to take advantage of the busier traffic. Free internet in each room (18 doubles) and kids under six stay free – this is not a bad deal at all.

Eden

Ciemna 15 (012 430 65 65/www. hoteleden.pl). Tram 3, 9, 11, 13, 24. **ZZ**.

Near the hub of Szeroka, this handy three-star houses a range of paid extras that you wouldn't find anywhere else in Krakow – a salt grotto (15zł) for respiratory ailments, for example. There's also a mikvah bath (7zł, non-guests 20zł), in-room Polynesian massages (140zł) and a sauna (25zł/hr). And, almost equally randomly, the Eden contains a sports pub, Ye Olde Goat, complemented by a kosher restaurant. The rooms themselves are pretty standard but well priced for the location – and amenities at hand.

ESSENTIALS

Backpacker heaven

Hostel Flamingo

'When we opened in 2006 there were 20 places in town,' said Pawel Wawro, head of the award-winning **Hostel Flamingo** (see p137). 'And now there are well over a hundred.' Pawel shouldn't worry. His spot on Szewska was one of two in Krakow to make Hostel World's global top ten for 2008 (the so-called 'Hoscars') – only Lisbon did better. Pawel's first-floor Flamingo is forever busy, its eight rooms, comfortable TV room and kitchen filled with backpackers delighted to be two minutes' walk from the main square and a one-minute stagger from a late-night bar strip.

Ten years ago, budget digs here meant a private room in an old lady's house or paying over the odds in an unrenovated flophouse by the station. Now 24-hour entry, hot power showers, free internet and clean kitchens are a given. Superior spots such as **Nathan's Villa Hostel** (see p141) also provide free laundry and films. The Flamingo lays on cultural walks and bar crawls.

Some venues throw in a gimmick to get ahead. Walk off the train from Prague and at the station is a red star and a sign with the name 'Lenin' – **Good Bye Lenin** hostels (www.goodbyelenin.pl) likes to get new recruits early. Decorated with Commie signs and posters, this themed lodging in Kazimierz offers a barbecue area and movie nights. Its branch in bucolic Zakopane boasts 'free squirrels, deers and bears'. The **Hostel Giraffe** (Krowoderska 31, 012 430 00 73, www.hostelgiraffe.com) features one in reception; the **Stranger** (Dietla 97, 012 432 09 09, www.thestranger-hostel.com) contains a Ju-Ju Lounge for party fun, and the **Secret Garden Hostel & Pension** (Skawinska 7, 012 430 54 45, www.thesecretgarden.pl) offers backpacking visitors greenery with a summer barbecue.

Ester

*Szeroka 20 (012 429 11 68/www.
hotel-ester.krakow.pl). Tram 3, 9, 11,
13, 24.* **ZZ**.
Location, location, location – and the
Ester is right on Szeroka. The public
areas are lovely and bright, including
the namesake restaurant, although
rooms can be a little on the small side,
some with quarter-moon bath/shower-
tubs. In some, views compensate. The
sauna, too, is boxy, but there are various massage treatments including ma-
uri, lomi-lomi and aromatherapy.

Kolory Bed & Breakfast

*Estery 10 (012 421 04 65/www.
kolory.com.pl). Tram 6, 8, 10.* **Z**.
Comfortable, cheap and conveniently
located, you won't get a better offer in
all Kazimierz than a stay in one of the
13 spacious rooms above Les Couleurs
bar slap on plac Nowy. A French-style
breakfast is taken in the French-style
café downstairs, where regulars read
the papers and check emails – which
you can also do in your room.

Nathan's Villa Hostel

*Św Agnieszki 1 (012 422 35 45/www.
nathansvilla.com). Tram 18, 19, 22.* **Z**.
A notch above most hostels in town,
with branches around Poland for those
who are interrailing. 'Designed by a
backpacker for backpackers,' goes its
motto, and it shows. NVH provides
powerful showers to cleanse the weari-
est of travellers, Wi-Fi, a pool table,
table tennis, surround-sound movies
and, best of all, free laundry. Nathan's
is not the best located of the city's backpacking bases, but Krakow is so compact it hardly matters.. See box p140.

Pugetów

*Starowiślna 15A (012 432 49 50/
www.donimirski.com). Tram 1, 3, 7,
13, 19, 24.* **ZZ**.
Set in a 19th-century palace inherited
by Jerzy Donimirski, owner of the local
boutique-hotel group of the same
name, the Pugetów is compact but
imaginatively conceived. Each of the
six units has been designed around a
historical figure: Pani Walewska,

Napoleon's famous lover, has been
characterised by a luxurious suite;
Joseph Conrad, a single room, and the
Pugets, an influential artistic family, a
triple. Accommodation is currently
being extended and guests may use the
quiet courtyard terrace for coffee and
postcard writing. See box p145.

Rubinstein

*Szeroka 12 (012 384 00 00/www.hotel
rubinstein.com). Tram 3, 9, 11, 13, 24.*
ZZZ.
The finest hotel in Kazimierz overlooks
Szeroka, a few doors down from where
the namesake cosmetician grew up.
The 22 rooms over seven floors are
done out with due taste, some with
original wooden ceilings from the 16th
and 17th centuries. The gym and sauna
are functional extras but don't miss out
on the roof terrace, perfect for an early-
evening drink. A top-quality restaurant is open to non-guests too.

Wawel & Waterfront

Hotel Poleski

NEW *Sandomierska 6 (012 260 54 05/
www.hotelpoleski.pl). Tram 18, 19.* **ZZ**.
Standard, clean and functional, the
recently opened Poleski, a rare find
across the river, beats most mid-range
competitors with its stellar view across
the Vistula and over to Wawel. It is one
shared by the notable first-floor restaurant, fourth-floor terrace and many of
the 20 rooms. Those without one are
about 15% cheaper.

Pod Wawelem

*Na Groblach 22 (012 426 26 25/www.
hotelpodwawelem.pl). Tram 1, 2, 6.* **ZZ**.
Those booking this regular internet
cheapie find themselves well located,
as the name implies, 'Below Wawel', in
a smallish, tidy room and equipped
with a small discount at underrated
cosmopolitan restaurant Lemonday
downstairs. Below is a small gym and
minuscule sauna but you'll be spend-
ing most of the time around Krakow's
historic sights a short walk away.
Handy stroll to the river too.

ESSENTIALS

HOTELS IN THE VERY CENTER OF KRAKÓW

Style and comfort,
20 rooms and 2 suites,
excellent cuisine,
cafe and bar,
sauna and fitness,
conference room.

20 MIKOŁAJSKA STREET, 31-027 KRAKÓW
TEL +48 12 429 60 70, FAX +48 12 429 60 62
amadeus@janpol.com.pl, www.hotel-amadues.pl

Modern interiors, 232 Standard, Classic
and Premium rooms, 5 conference rooms,
restaurant and lobby bar, souvenir gallery,
casino and parking.

15 WESTERPLATTE STREET, 31-033 KRAKÓW
TEL +48 12 422 95 66, FAX +48 12 422 57 19
wyspianski@janpol.com.pl, www.hotel-wyspianski.pl

Pugetów p141

Sheraton Kraków

Powiśle 7 (012 662 10 00/www. sheraton.com/krakow). Tram 1, 2, 6. **ZZZ**.
The landmark Sheraton asserts its individuality and attracts non-guests with its rather smart Olive restaurant, SomePlace Else sports bar and cocktail bar QUBE. Guests in the 232 rooms, done out to the usual Sheraton standards, can also use the heated pool with water jet, gym and saunas, separate for men and women, perhaps preferred that way by American visitors.

Podgórze & the South

Farmona Business Hotel & Spa

NEW *Jugowicka 10C (012 252 70 70/ www.farmonahotel.com). Bus 104.* **ZZ**.
A very impressive facility, this, although you are stuck quite a way out of town. Surrounded by trees and a pretty, spacious garden with gazebo, where you can take your hard-chosen, enticing breakfast spread, Farmona woos its peace-seeking guests with the

sound of trickling water, most notably in the Oriental spa. There guests flop in bathrobes, read or contemplate the greenery. Farmona hasn't quite got the hang of spas yet – someone has seen fit to sample jungle noises to frighten unsuspecting sauna users – but with Wi-Fi in all 30 rooms and an excellent contemporary restaurant in the Magnifica, this is a spot for complete relaxation and indulgence.

Qubus Hotel

NEW *Nadwiślańska 6 (012 374 51 00/ www.qubushotel.com). Tram 3, 9, 11, 13, 24.* **ZZ**.
This new business and spa hotel has been sited in grey Podgórze, right by the former Jewish Ghetto. The location, a short taxi hop or tram ride across the river from Kazimierz, doesn't seem so strange once you're bubbling away in the panoramic jacuzzi seven floors up, beside a pool and loungers high over the river. In fact, for the price (there are attractive internet deals), it's almost bargain luxury. Breakfast, taken in the commendable, light and spacious Ogień restaurant, is substantial, you

ESSENTIALS

can snack or sip cocktails in the Barracuda lobby bar and start the evening at the Mile Stone or After Work bars. You'll be looking for another online deal before you know it.

Kleparz & the North

andel's

Pawla 1 (012 660 01 00/www.andels cracow.com). ZZZ.

Slap opposite the station, part of the relandscaped complex also incorporating the Galeria Krakowska mall, this business hotel is swish, modern but all a bit functional, as if boxes were being ticked to satisfy standard demands. For all that, taking a decent breakfast in the Delight restaurant, sitting in the cabin-like sauna or completing their quota in the gym, guests in the 159 rooms are well looked after, a short walk from the Old Town and easy train hop from the airport.

Atrium

Krzywa 7 (012 430 02 03/www.hotel atrium.com.pl). Tram 3, 5. Z.

In a no-man's-land of hostels and grim two-stars, the three-star Atrium offers a slightly more comfortable stay in its 50 rooms and two self-catering apartments. Location is still its strongest point, although the courtyard is a pleasant place to start the day.

Basztowa Guesthouse

Basztowa 24 (012 429 51 81). Z.

Dead cheap this, particularly from November to March, centrally located near the station and the Old Town, and by no means uncomfortable. In fact, a number of worse three-stars could easily be mentioned. To offer this price, the Basztowa has had to do without a website and a receptionist – you collect your keys from the pricier Polonia next door. If all you need are a pillow and a short walk to all amenities, you won't be complaining here.

Europejski

Lubicz 5 (012 423 25 10/www.he.pl). Z.

In those grim old days just after the Changes, visitors to Krakow were faced with a strip of overpriced, unrenovated, turn-of-the-century hotels

Hotel Poleski p141

Redressing history

Maltański

Thanks to a random inheritance, Krakow has three high-end, boutique conversions of historic buildings, in or by the Old Town: **Donimirski Hotels**. Behind them is Jerzy Donimirski, a local architect who gained his experience in Poland, Germany and Los Angeles.

'I inherited the **Pugetów Palace** and began work on it after 1990,' said Jerzy. 'I had no idea of moving into hotels.' He renovated the 19th-century building as offices. 'In Germany I stayed in a historic property with modern-day facilities. I began thinking about adapting my own heritage building, to create something interesting.' Jerzy then acquired a 200-year-old house across the Old Town from the Pugetów, the **Maltański** (see p147). 'The property originally served as a local residence with garages for horse carriages. When we found it, it was a kindergarten but the ceilings and the roof were collapsing. Initially it was hard as our workers weren't used to top materials from the West.'

The Maltański, classy and cosy, was opened in 2000. The Pugetów (see p141), unveiled two years later, was more ambitious, each of the six units tastefully decorated by themed character: Napoleon's lover Pani Walewska, Joseph Conrad, and so on.

In 2005, came the **Gródek** (see p135), once part of a medieval convent. 'We used the maximum space without destroying the building's historic character,' said Jerzy. 'Detailed estoration was done by specialist craftsmen under constant supervision.'

The result is superb, the historic finds dug up by the team on display in the equally impressive restaurant, **Cul-de-Sac**. Rooms are comfort itself: heated bathroom floors, tubs where possible, free hot drinks and fluffy bathrobes.

New hotel projects include the **Dwór Kościuszko** manor, in Prądnik Biały park ten minutes' drive north of the centre; and, further ahead, the **Castle Korzkiew** just outside Krakow.

ESSENTIALS

Sheraton Kraków p143

opposite the station. This was one of them. Since then, although its old neon sign is still in place, the Europejski has been much improved, Jacek Czepczyk following in the footsteps of his grandfather who designed it a century ago.

Czarna Wieś & West

Art Hotel Niebieski

NEW *Flisacka 3 (012 431 18 58/www. niebieski.com.pl). Tram 1, 2, 6.* **ZZ**.
Work in progress best describes the Niebieski – a spa, underground parking and twice the number of rooms are promised by the autumn of 2009. In the meantime, this mid-range venue provides a comfortable home from home in the convenient locality of Salwator, three tramlines and ten minutes from the Old Town. Should you decide to stay put, it has a restaurant too – although rooms may not quite be up to the three-and-a-half star status the hotel has somehow awarded itself.

Cracovia

Al Focha 1 (012 424 56 00/www. orbis.pl). Tram 15, 18. **ZZ**.

Tour buses sit in the spacious car park outside the Cracovia, opposite the National Museum, ready to take visitors to Wieliczka and Auschwitz – this 300-plus-room hotel is a local landmark. The Cracovia is still a Polish-run Orbis, which is both comforting – many a uniform Mercure or Etap around Poland is now also in the same family – and frustrating when scores of low-paying guests are trying to check out at the same time. Young or old-school staff can also book myriad trips and sports activities (including skiing), all as paid extras.

Ibis Kraków Centrum

Syrkomil 2 (012 299 33 00/www. ibishotel.com). Tram 1, 2, 6. **Z**.
Handy location (near the river, pretty close to Wawel), great price and decent service – Krakow's 175-room Ibis cannot be gainsaid, really. Throw in recently installed flat-screen TVs, wide beds and a pleasant, expansive terrace café-restaurant, where breakfast is served from very early in the morning, and the undemanding individual visitor to Krakow is in business.

ESSENTIALS

Maltański

*Straszewskiego 14 (012 431 00 10/
www.donimirski.com). Tram 2, 3, 4,
12, 13, 14, 15, 18, 24.* **ZZZ**.

Peaceful and eminently comfortable,
this three-star in the Donimirski group
allows you to get away from it all yet
access the Old Town by the simple act
of crossing the road. It's all done by
means of a patio breakfast area, luxurious rooms with complimentary hot
drinks and heated bathroom floors,
and an intimate feel to the two floors
along which the 16 rooms are lined.
Almost a decade old now – this was the
Donimirski's first conversion – but
none the worse for it. See box p145.

Novotel Centrum

*Kościuszki 5 (012 299 29 00/www.
novotel.com). Tram 1, 2, 6.* **ZZ**.

Budget business travellers and families plot up at the Ibis Centrum – more
demanding ones are looked after at the
nearby Novotel. What they get, along
with the same riverside location, are a
heated pool, gym, jacuzzi and sauna
and, for some, a view of Wawel.

Attractive family-stay arrangements
(two kids under 16 stay and have
breakfast for free) are currently in place
– the safe-play area is a boon.

Ostoya Palace Hotel

*Piłsudskiego 24 (012 430 90 00/www.
ostoyapalace.pl). Tram 15, 18.* **ZZZ**.

The lesser-known of the historic hotel
conversions, 19th-century Ostaszewski
Palace, between the Old Town and the
verdant west, proves a fine framework
for 24 beautifully upholstered rooms.
There is a restaurant and bar too, with
a modest agenda of cultural events.

Radisson SAS

*Straszewskiego 17 (012 618 88 88/
www.radissonsas.com). Tram 2, 3, 4,
12, 13, 14, 15, 18, 24.* **ZZZ**.

Just across from the Old Town, this
Radisson has been opened recently
enough to mean that its gym has the
latest equipment, its bar and restaurant
(Milk&Co, Salt&Co) cater to contemporary tastes, and the overall look of the
196-room building feels light and new.
Work by local artists has been added
in each. Free broadband throughout.

Maltański

ESSENTIALS

Getting Around

By air

Balice airport
012 295 58 00/
www.krakowairport.pl.
About 15km (nine miles) west
of the city centre.

The quickest way to town is
to walk the short distance from
Arrivals down a slip road to the
right as you exit the building,
to the platform for regular trains
(4.30am-midnight daily, 6zł) to
Krakow main station. Buy tickets
on board, journey time 15 minutes.
An infrequent free shuttle bus also
serves the platform from Balice.
The slow local bus No.292 takes
the long route to town (for fares,
see p149 **Public transport**).

A taxi should cost about 70zł –
fares rise steeply after 10pm.
Reliable cabs park outside Arrivals.

The following airlines currently
have a direct service from the UK
to Krakow:

British Airways
0844 493 0787/from Poland
+800 441 1592/www.ba.com.
From London Gatwick.

easyJet
0871 244 2366/in Poland 0703
203 025/www.easyjet.com.
From Belfast International, Bristol,
Edinburgh, Liverpool, London
Gatwick, London Luton and
Newcastle.

Jet2
0871 226 1737/from Poland
+44 203 031 8103.
From Leeds-Bradford.

LOT
0845 601 0949/in Poland
0801 703 703/from Polish
mobile 229 572/www.lot.com.
From London Heathrow.

Ryanair
0871 246 0000/in Poland 0703
303 033/www.ryanair.com.
From Birmingham, East Midlands,
Edinburgh, Glasgow, Liverpool and
London Stansted.

Wizzair
0904 475 9500/in Poland 0703
503 010/www.wizzair.com.
Serves 'Katowice/Cracow' from
Doncaster-Sheffield, Glasgow
Prestwick, Liverpool and London
Luton.

Katowice airport (www.gtl.
com.pl) is 90 minutes' drive away.
Wizzair runs buses (www.turysta.
com.pl) to Krakow city centre.
Krakow Shuttle (www.krakow
shuttle.com) runs a service for both
Katowice and Krakow airports, to
and from Krakow city centre.

By rail

Polish railways
www.pkp.pl.
Polish trains are affordable
and generally reliable. There is
a buffet bar on Intercity services
(www.intercity.pl). You can buy
tickets online. The inland
information service is on 0801 022
007. Outside Poland dial +48 422
055 007. The independent website
www.polrail.com is also useful.

There are regular connections
with Warsaw, fastest journey time
3hrs. Two services a day run from
Berlin (10hrs), Vienna (6-8hrs) and
Budapest (9hrs), including
an overnight service from each.

Main-line station

Dworzec Główny
Krakow main station
Pl Jana Nowaka-Jeziorańskiego
3 (012 393 15 80/
www.rozklad.pkp.pl).

The main station is just outside the Old Town to the north-east. It's a ten-minute walk to the main square. Ticket queues can be long, so either buy online or from the Orbis office on the main square (Rynek Główny 41, 012 619 24 59, www.orbis.krakow.pl).

By bus

Dworzec autobusowy
Krakow bus station
Bosacka 18 (012 393 52 52/ www.rda.krakow.pl).
The swish new bus terminus is just behind the train station – it's signposted along the warren of underground passages.

Public transport

Krakow city transport (www.mpk. krakow.pl) consists of trams and buses. Services run from 5am to 11pm then a number of night buses take over. Tickets are sold at kiosks by stops, 2.50zł for a single journey, 3.10zł for one hour and 10.40zł for 24 hours. Longer passes and family weekend tickets are also available. Tickets are 0.50zł more expensive to buy from the driver. Stamp your ticket immediately after you board. The **Krakow Card** (see below) allows free transport for the validity of the pass.

Krakow Card

The **Krakow Card** (www.krakow card.com) is valid for 30 museums, for free travel on trams, buses and nightbuses, and for discounts at certain local shops and restaurants, as well as for a few excursions. It comes in two-day (50zł) and three-day (65zł) varieties and is sold at 20 tourist information offices and travel agencies across the city, at a dozen hotels, and via www.symposium.pl/index.php.

Taxis

Most local taxis are reliable these days and feature an illuminated company sign on the roof. Do make sure that the driver turns on the meter. You'll find taxis outside the main station, on certain streets (Sienna, Szewska) off the main market square, and on the corner of plac Nowy and Estery in the nightlife hub of Kazimierz. Firms include **Radio Taxi** (012 9191), **City Taxi** (012 9621) and **Euro Taxi** (012 9664).

Driving

The only motorway into Krakow is the busy A4 toll one from Katowice. If you're driving from the UK, you will need the registration documents of your vehicle, your international insurance green card and your driving licence.

It is compulsory to wear belts in the front and back seats and to equip the car with rear-wheel mud flaps. Children under 12 must sit in the back. In winter, headlights must be switched on at all times.

The limit of alcohol in the blood for drivers is 0.2, the equivalant of a small glass of beer or wine. Polish speed limits are 60kph in built-up areas, 90kph on country roads, 120kph on dual carriageways and 130kph on motorways.

At garages, unleaded fuel is labelled *benzyna bezolowiowa*. Traffic drives on the right.

Vehicle removal

The **national breakdown emergency** number is 9637. The **Polish Motoring Association** also runs a breakdown service (022 849 9361, www.pzm.pl). Towing away is charged by the kilometre unless you are insured against breakdowns.

ESSENTIALS

Resources A-Z

Accident & emergency

The main emergency number is 999 or 112 if called from a mobile. If you need the fire brigade the number is 998 and for the police, 997. For medical advice 24/7 call 012 661 22 40 or 9439. EU nationals should receive free medical treatment if they are carrying a European Health Insurance Card but this may mean having to pay in advance and reclaim the money later. Bureaucracy can be a hindrance and it is always worth investing in travel insurance.

John Paul II Hospital *Pradnicka 80 (012 614 20 00/www.szpitaljp2. krakow.pl).*
Main hospital in Krakow, opened in 1997.

Old Town Clinic *pl Świętego Ducha 3 (012 422 1771).*
The most central of Krakow's walk-in clinics (*przychodnia*).

Medicover *Rakowicka 7 (0804 229 596/0411 9596/hotline 19677/www.medicover.com/plpl/).*
Open 7am-11pm Mon-Fri; 8am-2pm Sat.
The most well known of Krakow's international private clinics.

Credit card loss

American Express
012 423 1202/www.american express.com/poland.
Diners Club
022 826 0766/www.dinersclub.pl.
Mastercard
+1 800 627 8372/www. mastercard.com/plp.
Visa
+1 800 111 1569/ www.visaeurope.com.

Customs

As Poland is in the European Union, there are no restrictions on bringing in or taking out duty-paid goods for personal use – except cigarettes, limited to 200 per person. Coming in from outside the EU, the allowances are 200 cigarettes or 250 grams of tobacco; one litre of spirits or two litres of wine; two litres of fortified or sparkling wine. Non-EU citizens may claim back the VAT tax of 22% on goods bought in Poland within three months of purchase from shops carrying stickers 'Tax Free Shopping'. Global Refund Polska (www.globalrefund.com) can sort out the paperwork.

Poland operates a very strict policy on the export of goods (artworks, books, furniture) made before 1945 – officially classified as antiques.

Dental emergency

Denta-Med
Augustiańska 13 (012 430 60 76); Na Zjeżdzie 13 (012 259 80 00). For both, www.denta-med.com.pl.

Disabled

The cobblestone streets of the Old Town and most city trams are not wheelchair-friendly. Some hotels and museums, and the train station, are adapted for wheelchair access.

Electricity

Electricity is 220 volts with two-pin plugs used everywhere. UK visitors should bring continental adaptors with them as they are expensive in Poland – if available at all.

Embassies & consulates

The following provide consular support within Krakow but cannot offer full visa or passport services:

UK Consulate
Św Anny 9 (012 421 70 30/ www.fco.gov.uk).

US Consulate
Stolarska 9 (012 424 51 00/ http://krakow.usconsulate.gov).

For visa and passport assistance within Poland, all the following offices are in Warsaw:

Australian Embassy
Nowgrodzka 11 (022 521 34 44/ www.poland.embassy.gov.au).
Open 9am-5pm Mon-Fri.

British Embassy
Warsaw Corporate Centre Emilii Plater 28 (022 625 30 30/ http://ukinpoland.fco.gov.uk).
Open 8.30am-2pm Mon, Tue, Thur, Fri; 8.30am-noon Wed.

Canadian Embassy
Jana Matejki 1/5 (022 584 31 00/ www.Poland.ga.ca). **Open** 8.30am-4.30pm Mon-Fri.

Irish Embassy
Mysia 5 (022 849 66 33/ www.embassyofireland.pl).
Open 9am-1pm, 2-5pm Mon-Fri.

US Embassy
Al Ujazdowskie 29-31 (022 504 20 00/http://poland.usembassy.gov).
Open 10am-noon, 2-4pm Mon-Fri.

Internet

Central Krakow has an abundance of internet cafés – there are three on Floriańska alone. Hourly fees are modest and most also offer printing and other services. Empik (p68) is also a popular spot to check your emails on the main square.

Garinet
Floriańska 18 (012 423 22 33/ www.garinet.pl). **Open** 9am-midnight daily.

Money

The unit of currency in Poland is still the złoty. In October 2008, the Polish government confirmed its intention to introduce the euro by 2012. Until that time, the złoty will be in everyday use. Złotys come in notes of 200, 100, 50, 20 and ten, and coins of five, two and one.

Złotys are divided into 100 groszy. You'll still be handed a 50 groszy coin, perhaps the odd 20 but lower denominations are hardly used these days.

The current rate of exchange is 5.3zł to the pound sterling, 4.7zł to the euro and 3.75zł to the dollar. Money can be changed at banks and hotels but you will get a better rate at one of the many exchange bureaux (*kantor*) around the Old Town. Rates are clearly displayed and no commission should be charged on the transaction.

ATMs are everywhere in town with at least half-a-dozen on the main market square alone.

Opening hours

Offices in Poland open at 9am and close at 5pm, Mondays to Fridays. Banks usually operate from 8am to 5pm, Mondays to Saturdays.

Police

For emergencies, *see* **Accident & emergencies**.
Central Police Station
Rynek Główny 29 (012 615 7317).

Post

The main post office is just east of the Old Town on the Planty ring.
Poczta Główna
Westerplatte 20 (012 421 03 48/ www.poczta-polska.pl). **Open** 7.30am-8.30pm Mon-Fri; 8am-2pm Sat.

ESSENTIALS

Smoking

Although more and more cafés and restaurants are going smoke-free around Krakow, smoking is not entirely prohibited here. Local campaigns such as Lokal Bez Papierosa are trying to raise public awareness and have smoking barred from dining and drinking establishments. For the time being, you can expect non-smoking areas in the city's better restaurants – and cellars thick with smoke when it comes to barhopping.

Telephones

The dialling code for Poland is 48. If you're calling from outside the country dial your international access code (in the case of the UK, it's 00), then 48, followed by the city code.

The city code for Krakow is 012, which you have to dial when you are inside Poland. Also within the city itself, dial the 012 first. Outside Poland, dial +48 12 followed by the seven-digit phone number.

Mobile numbers in Poland are ten digits and usually start with 05, 06, 07 or 08. Calling a Polish mobile from the UK or in Poland from a UK mobile can be expensive. The mobile numbers in this guide are indicated as such for that reason.

Public phones

Public phones operate with phonecards (karty telefoniczne) sold in units of 15, 30 and 60 from post offices and newsstands. You can also call from main post offices; see p151 Post.

Tickets

The Empik (p68) media store on the main market square is the best one-stop outlet for tickets for major rock and classical concerts. The downtown City Information Point (Św Jana 2, 012 421 77 87, www.karnet-krakow.pl), run by the same people behind the leading arts information monthly *Karnet*, is the best source for tickets for theatre, dance and classical events.

Time

Poland is on Central European Time (CET), one hour ahead of the UK. Like the UK, clocks change by one hour in October and March.

Tipping

Poles round up restaurant bills and taxi charges to around ten per cent of the overall fee. Tipping is not expected in bars and cafés unless you have had exceptional service.

Tourist information

The main city tourist office is on a patch of green Planty between the train station and the Old Town. There is a regional one in the Cloth Hall on the main market square.
Tourist Information Centre
Szpitalna 25 (012 432 01 10/00 60/www.biurofestiwalowe.pl).
Open *Winter* 9am-5pm daily. *Summer* 9am-7pm daily.
Małopolska Tourist Information
Sukiennice, Rynek Główny 1/3 (012 421 77 06/www.mcit.pl).
Open 9am-5pm daily.

Visas

EU, US, Canadian and Australian nationals need no visa for Poland.

What's on

Events details can be found via www.Cracow-Life.com and its free leaflet www.e-krakow.com. *Karnet* monthly is handy too; see **Tickets**.

Vocabulary

Polish is the most popular West Slavic language and is the mother tongue of all but three per cent of the population of Poland.

Like other Slav languages, it is highly inflected, which means the endings of words may change depending on their role in the sentence. *Gazeta* is newspaper but it's *gazetę* if you're buying one. The language has three genders and seven cases. Like other Slav languages, there is no word for 'a' or 'the' – it needs to be worked out from the context.

Word order is flexible. You may put a word at the start of the sentence for emphasis.

Phrases below refer to a man if 'Pan' and a woman if 'Pani'.

Pronunciation

Polish has eight vowels (two nasal) and every letter is pronounced. The stress is on the second-to-last syllable. Accents alter the sound of the sibilant consonants – from *z* to *ż* and so on.

ą nasal 'on' as in French *on*.
c 'ts' as in cats.
cz, ć 'ch' as in cheese.
dz, dż 'j' as in jam.
ę 'en' as in envelope.
ł 'w' as in wave.
ń 'ni' as in onion.
ó 'oo' as in took.
rz 's' as in treasure.
sz, ś 'sh' as in shoes.
w 'v' as in vulgar.
ż 's' as in pleasure.

Basics

Yes *tak* 'tak'
No *nie* 'nyeh'
Please *proszę* 'prosheh'
Thank you *dziękuję* 'djenkooyeh'
You're welcome *proszę* 'prosheh'
Hello *cześć* 'cheshch'
Good day *dzień dobry* 'djyen' dobri'
Good evening *dobry wieczór* 'dobri vye-chur'
Good night *dobranoc* 'dobranots'
Goodbye *do widzenia* 'do veed-zen-ya'

Useful phrases

Excuse me *proszę Pana/Pani* 'prosheh pana/pani'
Sorry! *przepraszam!* 'psheprasham'
How are you? *Jak się Pan/Pani miewa?* 'yak siye pan/pani myeva'
Very well, thank you *dobrze, dziękuję* 'dobjeh djenkooyeh'
I don't understand. *Nie rozumiem* 'nyeh rozoo-yem'
Do you speak English? *Czy mówi Pan/Pani po angielsku?* 'chi moo-vee pan/pani po ang-yel-skoo'
I can't speak Polish. *Nie mówię po polsku* 'nyeh moo-yeh po polskoo'
I don't know. *Nie wiem* 'nyeh vyem'
Please speak more slowly. *Proszę mówić wolniej* 'prosheh moo-veech voln-yay'
My name is... *Nazywam się...* 'nazivam sheh'
Can I have...? *Poproszę...?* 'poprosheh'
How much is it? *Ile kosztuje?* 'ee-leh kosh-tooye'
When? *Kiedy?* 'ki-yedi'
What? *Co takiego?* 'tso tak-yego'
There is (Is there?) *Czy jest?* 'chi yest'
Where is the toilet? *Gdzie jest toaleta?* 'gjeh yest to-aleta'
Cheers! *Na zdrowie!* 'na zdrov-yeh'

Signs

Toalety toilets
Dla pań gentlemen
Dla panów ladies

Otwarte open
Zamknięte closed
Wejście entrance
Wyjście exit
Pchnąć push
Ciągnąć pull
Uwaga! attention!, look out!
Wstęp wzbroniony no entry
Ciepła hot
Zimna cold

Directions

Where is...? *Gdzie jest....?* 'gjeh yest'
To the right *Na prawo* 'na pravo'
To the left *Na lewo* 'na levo'
Is it very far? *Czy to jest bardzo daleko?* 'chi to yest bardzo daleko'
The station *dworzec* 'dvo-zets'
Platform *peron* 'peron'
Train *pociąg* 'pochawng'
Ticket *bilet* 'beelet'
A single/return ticket to... please *Proszę bilet w jedną stronę/ powrotny bilet do...* 'prosheh beelet v yednawn stroneh/ povrotni beelet do'

Time

What time is it? *Która jest godzina?* 'ktoora yest god-zina'
Late *późno* 'poojno'
Early *wcześnie* 'vcheshn-yeh'
Soon *nie długo* 'nyeh dwoogo'
Today *dzisiaj* 'jee-shay'
Yesterday *wczoraj* 'vchoray'
Tomorrow *jutro* 'yutro'
Tonight *dzisiejszej nocy* 'jee-shay-shay notsi'
Next week *w przyszłym tygodniu* 'vpshishwim ti-godn-yoo'

Days & months

Monday *poniedziałek* 'pon-yejawek'
Tuesday *wtorek* 'vtorek'
Wednesday *środa* 'shroda'
Thursday *czwartek* 'chvartek'
Friday *piątek* 'p-yawn-tek'
Saturday *sobota* 'sobota'
Sunday *niedziela* 'nyeh-jela'

January *styczeń* 'stichen-yuh'
February *luty* 'looti'
March *marzec* 'maryets'
April *kwiecień* 'kv-yechen-yuh'
May *maj* 'mayets'
June *czerwiec* 'cherv-yets'
July *lipiec* 'leep-yets'
August *sierpień* 'sherp-yen-yuh'
September *wrzesień* 'vjeshen-yuh'
Octo ber *październik* 'paj-jerneek'
November *listopad* 'leestopad'.
December *grudzień* 'groojen-yuh'

Numbers

0 *zero* 'zero'
1 *jeden* 'yeden'
2 *dwa* 'dva'
3 *trzy* 'tshi'
4 *cztery* 'chteri'
5 *pięć* 'pi-yench'
6 *sześć* 'shesh'
7 *siedem* 'shye-dem'
8 *osiem* 'oshem'
9 *dziewięć* 'jev-yench'
10 *dziesięć* 'jesh-yench'
11 *jedenaście* 'yedenash-cheh'
12 *dwanaście* 'dvanash-cheh'
13 *trzynaście* 'tshinash-cheh'
14 *czternaście* 'chternash-cheh'
15 *piętnaście* 'pyont-nash-cheh'
16 *szesnaście* 'shes-nash-cheh'
17 *siedemnaście* 'shyedemnash-cheh'
18 *osiemnaście* 'oshemnash-cheh'
19 *dziewiętnaście* 'jev-yent-nash-cheh'
20 *dwadzieścia* 'dva-jesh-cha'
30 *trzydzieści* 'tshijesh-chi'
40 *tzterdzieści* 'chter-jesh-chi'
50 *pięćdziesiąt* 'pyench-jeshawnt'
60 *sześćdziesiąt* 'sheshjeshawnt'
70 *siedemdziesiąt* 'shyedem-jeshawnt'
80 *osiemdziesiąt* 'oshem-jeshawnt'
90 *dziewięćdziesiąt* 'jev-yench-jeshawnt'
100 *sto* 'sto'
200 *dwieście* 'dvyesh-cheh'
500 *pięćset* 'pyench-set'
1,000 *tysiąc* 'teeshawnts'
1,000,000 *milion* 'meelyon'

Menu Glossary

Meals

Breakfast *śniadanie*
Lunch *obiad*
Dinner *kolacja*

Courses

Zupy soups
Przekąski starters
Dania drugie main courses
Dodatki side dishes
Desery desserts
Napoje drinks

Useful words

Bill *rachunek* 'rahoonek'
Cup *filiżanka* 'filijanka'
Glass *szklanka* 'shklanka'
Plate *talerz* 'taley'
Serviette *serwetka* 'servetka'
Salt *sól* 'sool'
Menu *jadłospis* 'jadwo-spees'
Knife *nóż* 'nooj'
Fork *widelec* 'vee-delets'
Spoon *łyżka* 'wijka'
Teaspoon *łyżeczka* 'wee-jech-ka'
Milk *mleko* 'mleko'
Sugar *cukier* 'tsoo-kir'
Ashtray *popielnicza* 'popyelnichka'

Useful phrases

A table for one, please. *Stolik dla jednej osoby, proszę* 'stoleek dla yednay osobi prosheh'
A table for two, please. *Stolik dla dwóch osób, proszę* 'stoleek dla dvooh osoob prosheh'
What would you recommend? *Co Pan/Pani poleca?* 'tso pan/pani poletsa'
The bill, please. *Proszę rachunek* 'prosheh rahoonek'
I'd like... *Proszę...* 'prosheh'
I didn't order this! *Tego nie zamawiałem!* 'tego nyeh zamav-yawem'

Food types

Gotowany boiled
Nadziewany stuffed
Smażony fried
Z rusztu grilled
Chleb bread
Drób poultry
Dziczyzna game
Jarzyny/warzywa vegetables
Kapuszta cabbage
Kurczak chicken
Mięso meat
Potrawy jarskie vegetarian dishes
Pstrąg trout
Ryby fish
Ryż rice
Śledź herring
Wierprzowe pork
Ziemniaki potatoes

Dishes

Barszcz beetroot soup
Bigos hunter's stew
Gołąbki stuffed cabbage
Golonka pork leg with horseradish
Grzyby forest mushrooms
Naleśniki pancakes
Pierogi dough parcels
Żurek rye soup

Desserts

Ciastko cake
Lody ice-cream
Owoce fruit
Sernik cheesecake

Drinks

Herbata tea
Kawa coffee
Piwo beer
Sok juice
Wino wine
Woda water
Wódka vodka

ESSENTIALS

Index

Sights & Areas

ESSENTIALS

ESSENTIALS

Shopping

Nightlife

ESSENTIALS